Praise for

True Grit and Grace

I just read your book in one big gulp. Enthralling, entertaining, and heartfelt. You are a fine writer and you conveyed your life and your message with conviction and purpose. For the past twenty-five years, I have invested in people like you, with depth of character. You have iron in your core and a wise heart. In our search for happiness we are entitled to receive only that which we are prepared to give. Life has taught us that we get not what we deserve but what we expect. We are not what we say, or how we feel, or what we think. We are what we do. Congratulations on an outstanding book.

~ **Donald A. Wiss MD**

It's riveting. You have nailed the art of storytelling. I find your style of writing and the technique of going back and forth between your history and your accident/recovery extremely effective. You link the core of who you are with how you had the wherewithal to fight and overcome (an understatement, I know) are the catalyst for writing the book, but your story and your message are bigger than the accident. Your book isn't just another "I had a tragedy and I rose above it" story. Yours is about mindset for making life matter, for being "more" for being able to see the value and the opportunity in yourself *and* others. It's about thinking in terms of solutions, and *never* about benefiting from pity. Anyone who knew you before the accident had to know there was no way in the world the injury would ever derail you.

~ **Fay Taragan,** Independent Education Consultant

What a privilege it is to read this book. In one sitting, I chuckled, shed tears....and was joyfully uplifted. Amberly shares her story with an open heart, exposing her vulnerabilities while progressing forward with each challenge. I am profoundly transformed by her spirit, honesty, and example: to embrace life, persevere, forgive, and evolve, and find the gem in even the toughest of circumstances. She motivates with clarity and truth and inspires positivity.

~ **Debbie Norton,** Senior Vice President Production
Sony Pictures and Television

Amberly is one of the bravest women I know. More than her courage, what I admire most is how she handles adversity—and her positive attitude that I'm sure has kept her alive and thriving. I can't even imagine dealing with the surgeries, setbacks, and adjustments that Amberly has. *True Grit and Grace* will pull you in like any great movie. It's a page turner. And knowing this is a true story, you'll be inspired and motivated to be grateful for your life. I know I was.

~ **Deborah Shames**, Author and Speaker

True Grit and Grace is an amazing journey of a truly courageous woman. Amberly is a natural storyteller. I was so touched with the honesty, vulnerability, and human connection in her writing. Her trials and tribulations are an inspiration to us all.

~ **Alison Eastwood,** Actress, Director and Animal Advocate

True Grit and Grace is a beautiful memoir illustrating how difficult experiences and deep wounds, both mental an physical, are the very things that can gift us a deeper power and resilience if we allow them to. Amberly generously brings us on her personal journey and shares her formula for moving through adversity and tremendous pain:

Grit + Grace = Resilience.

~ **Sonia Faye**, Energy Therapist

TRUE GRIT and *Grace*

TURNING TRAGEDY INTO TRIUMPH

Amberly Lago

NEW YORK

NASHVILLE • MELBOURNE • VANCOUVER • LONDON

True Grit and Grace

Turning Tragedy Into Triumph

Published in New York, New York, by Morgan James Publishing. Morgan James
is a trademark of Morgan James, LLC. www.MorganJamesPublishing.com

The Morgan James Speakers Group can bring authors to your live event. For
more information or to book an event visit The Morgan James Speakers Group
at www.TheMorganJamesSpeakersGroup.com.

ISBN 9781683506232 paperback
ISBN 9781683506249 eBook
Library of Congress Control Number: 2017945545

Cover Design by: Rachel Lopez

 www.r2cdesign.com

Book Design by: Glen M. Edelstein

www.hudsonvalleybookdesign.com

In an effort to support local communities, raise awareness and funds, Morgan
James Publishing donates a percentage of all book sales for the life of each book
to Habitat for Humanity Peninsula and Greater Williamsburg.

Get involved today! Visit
www.MorganJamesBuilds.com

Contents

Dedication

For my husband Johnny, who holds my
hand and has my heart.

For my daughters Savanna and Ruby Lee,
my biggest inspirations.

Introduction

LIFE CAN CHANGE IN A MOMENT. Everybody knows that, right? Everybody knows your fate, your destiny, your future can be transformed in the snap of a finger.

Sometimes that moment is a positive—say, meeting the love of your life in the produce section, or winning the lottery. Most often, though, we associate life-altering events with something catastrophic.

But if you think about it hard enough and long enough and clearly enough, you realize your whole life is, in a way, an accident. It's the result of a succession of whims, flukes, and quirks of fate. How your parents met. Where you lived. The schools you attended and the friends you met. What you were exposed to and interested in, and what you decided to do with those interests. The mentors who found you, or the ones you never found. Where you happened to be when you met your soulmate—or where you haven't been yet to meet that love of your life.

Almost everything about you and how you define yourself is seemingly a matter of happenstance. Even the big, hard choices you make between A and B; those, too, are a product of all the billion little decisions you made from a trillion little options that went into you being you. After all, you wouldn't be in a position to make those hard choices if you hadn't made countless previous ones.

No, this isn't rocket science. But compared to the complexity of human beings who don't always act in their own best interests—maybe because they've never sat down to analyze what their best interests are—rocket science isn't rocket science either.

As it happens, it took a catastrophic, life-changing accident for me to take a hard, careful look at my life—where I'd been, where I was going, what I valued most, and what I wanted my life to look like. So while it was an authentic catastrophe, it turned out to be anything but catastrophic. Through it, I developed a perspective on my life, the kind of perspective you can't get except by looking from the outside in, that has helped me think more clearly.

Obviously, I don't recommend enduring such a catastrophe before taking stock. What I do recommend is going to school on the lessons of others (me, for instance) and recognizing that your life is constructed like an endless array of dominoes, its pattern designed in such a way as to be otherwise invisible to you, and that if you don't like where you, or where the dominoes, are heading, you have the power to stop, reevaluate, reorient, and reconfigure.

Ever since I recovered sufficiently to casually talk about my experiences, I found that people are genuinely moved by what I have to say. At first I thought they were being polite. Then others who'd heard from others asked me to tell them my story directly, and soon I was being asked to speak in front of assembled crowds.

I promise you, no one could've been more surprised by the emotional reaction—both during, as judging by their faces, and later, when I'd receive letters and emails describing how "inspiring" my story had been—than I was. That's when I realized I needed to sit down and tell the whole thing from beginning to end.

While this isn't, per se, a self-help book, if you stick with me I think you can walk away from the reading with a new appreciation for your own power to create the kind of life you want and to appreciate the kind of life you have, even when external circumstances narrow your possibilities.

As someone once told me, "You've got a shovel in your hand. You can either lean on it and pray for a hole, or you can start digging."

1

In a Flash

MY HUSBAND JOHNNY AND I, ALONG with our daughter Ruby, live in a suburb of Los Angeles. Our house is off a state highway that begins at the beach and ascends up a mountain and winds through a canyon. It then emerges from the mountains and spills onto a long straightaway that ends at the base of some other mountains, for a total distance of twenty miles. We live about midway, at the point in which cars heading south no longer have to contend with red lights on their way into the canyon, for what can best be described as *Mr. Toad's Wild Ride.* Any traffic cop who wanted to make his daily quota of speeding tickets would have only to hide on one of the leafy side streets to catch, if he could, a hundred speeders an hour. It's a forty-five mile-per-hour zone, but you're likely to get honked at and tailgated if you go that slowly. I've seen cars going seventy; faster, even.

But it's not the speed that makes the road dangerous. It's that drivers making left turns have to do so from the regular left lane. Neither L.A. City nor L.A. County has seen fit to restripe the street with left-turn lanes around there. Since the vast majority of streets elsewhere in the city and county have them, they're something that most people expect to be there. In fact, left-turn lanes are at most intersections both north or south of where we live. That's why you get a lot of accidents with drivers in the left lane who, after realizing they're stuck behind a car waiting for oncoming traffic to pass before completing the turn, suddenly swerve into the right lane, where they're clipped by other cars going too fast.

Several years ago, I was heading south in my Dodge Charger and stopped to make a left turn onto our street, dutifully waiting for the oncoming traffic to pass. I considered jamming it to beat this one oncoming car but didn't because Ruby, my then one-year-old daughter, was in her car seat in the back.

One of the oddities of life is that sometimes we're punished for *not* doing the *wrong* thing—in this case, not turning in front of the oncoming car, a turn I know with a hundred percent certainty I would've made without hurting or damaging either car or their occupants.

WHAM!

A car going at least fifty-five crashed into the back of my Charger, sending us skidding into oncoming traffic that then had to skid to avoid hitting us. My car was totaled, but thank God, Ruby was unhurt. And for a while I thought I was too.

The noise of the crash was so loud, several of my neighbors ran out of their houses onto the boulevard, where now no cars were moving. One of those neighbors called Johnny. He was still a California Highway Patrol lieutenant then, and as soon he heard what had happened, he came flying over on his motorcycle.

John Lago is a big man—about six-four, two-twenty—and in his uniform with knee-high leather boots is an imposing figure. I think the Hulk himself would be intimidated by Johnny, dressed like that, walking toward him. The punk who'd whacked me sure was. He admitted he'd been texting and didn't have insurance, and pleaded with Johnny, "Don't hit me, don't kill me, don't hurt me. Please!" It was pathetic, especially because Johnny had no intention of hitting, nor had he intimated in any way that he planned to do so (even though he probably wanted to).

In the meantime, the paramedics had come to check on Ruby and me. Ruby, they declared, was fine. But they couldn't release me because my blood pressure was sky high. For someone like me, who's not only fit but professionally fit, with ordinary blood pressure of 100/60, 200/100 was justifiable cause for alarm.

Nonetheless I shouted, "You don't understand, I have to get home and feed my daughter! It's dinnertime; she needs to eat!"

That's all I was thinking about. Me, I'm always fine. I'm tough. I train people for a living and hadn't missed a day of working out myself, in sickness and in health and in crisis and in grief, for more years than I could remember.

They let me go. But the next morning I woke feeling like a team of ninja elves had broken in overnight and each taken a sledgehammer to a different body part. Still, I was up and out of the house before six to begin training my clients at the gym, with appointments scheduled on the hour all day. I made it through the first two clients without much trouble, but at nine o'clock one of my clients who'd been with me for years and knew me well came in. She didn't know what had happened, but apparently didn't need to know. After taking one look at me she said, "You're not well. You need to go home."

That I didn't argue with her meant I knew she was right. Everything hurt. Literally every part of my body. I couldn't get away from the pain that kept increasing by the minute, or so it seemed. Somebody told me that you don't really know for twenty-four hours after a trauma how your body is going to feel, and that's pretty much how this went. By late that afternoon, a full day after the accident, I had to accept the most strenuous thing I'd be able to do for the foreseeable future was call my clients to postpone their next appointments, and then the ones after that, and the ones after that.

Anyway, that was my reluctant plan. But by the next morning, I could tell I'd reached peak pain—it wouldn't be worse than this—and decided I could live with it enough to train my clients, even if I couldn't work out myself. For goodness sake, I had a living to make. We were a two-income family with two kids, and the disability insurance for personal trainers paid me merely a pittance.

For two months, aside from the pleasure of working and seeing my clients do what I wanted to be doing myself, I was miserable and grumpy. For me, inactivity is torture—and forced inactivity makes it gruesome. I can't sit still. Never could. Never wanted to. Never wanted to want to. So on my first day back working out after those two months, I wanted to ascertain exactly how much muscle mass I'd lost, something I couldn't determine until I began lifting. I also needed to gauge how badly my cardio system had suffered in the two months I couldn't run.

It was a Friday, the Friday beginning Memorial Day weekend 2010. May 28. I felt like a kid on Christmas morning as I put on my new, hot pink Lululemon jacket and black leggings. Instead of driving my car, I opted for riding my motorcycle, a gorgeous, jet-black 1200cc Harley Nightster, and stuffed all my personal belongings into Johnny's brand-new backpack that was lying on the couch.

I realize now it was kind of a foolishly *macha* thing, trying to prove to myself that I was back big-time. But you know how it is. On the ten-minute drive from my house to the gym

I sang as if I'd just been sprung from jail. It was all I could do not to shout *Yee-haw!* as I rode.

I trained clients till noon, then worked out with my workout partner, another trainer—a male. I'd never had a female workout partner because I love competing with the guys, insisting they work with me as hard as if they were going up against another testosterone-filled partner. Our usual routine was to do weights for an hour, then run— anywhere from five to ten miles in a giant loop around that part of the city.

As I lifted weights I could tell I'd lost some strength, but I also sensed I'd get it back quickly, if only on sheer will alone.

But running was a surprise. We did eleven miles in my best time ever, despite pain from a giant knot in my calf that had formed after mile five. I kept telling myself I didn't care about the pain, that I cared only about running and making him keep up with me, as opposed to the other way around.

On most of our runs we would normally chitchat; not about anything serious, just whatever might be going on in our lives. This time, though, we ran mostly in silence. There would've been a lot to say, since we hadn't done this in two months, but I needed to keep my concentration in order not to be distracted by the leg pain. Besides, this happened to be a gorgeous Southern California day, the kind people move here for, ever since the folks back in Iowa saw the New Year's Day photos of the Rose Parade and decided they'd had enough snow. We did the eleven miles in an hour six, meaning we averaged six minutes a mile—a blistering pace for anyone other than professional runners, though come to think of it I was, in a way, a professional runner. Nike had been paying me a stipend and giving me shoes to promote their new line of shoes by pacing runners' groups, and I was looking forward to picking that up again, now that I was well.

Afterward we drank some water, caught our breath, and toweled off the sweat. Showering at home would be better than at the gym, and besides, I was eager to get there and begin the long weekend with Johnny and the girls, swimming in the pool and firing up the barbecue.

I remember every moment of what came next as if it were a documentary film playing on an endless loop. I've rerun the whole scene in my mind hundreds of times, knowing that a single tiny incident, or one second faster or slower, would have changed the outcome.

I put on my helmet and jacket and Johnny's new backpack that now contained a pulled pork sandwich a client had given me; I was going to share it with him when he got home. The cycle seat was warm from the sun, and I sat for two extra seconds, enjoying it before turning the key that immediately brought the engine to life and sent my adrenaline coursing, as it always did whenever I anticipated riding.

A coworker called out to me. I didn't hear what she said, so I lifted my helmet a few inches.

"Be careful," she said.

"I will," I said, revving the engine.

What a great noise. I revved it three more times, just to hear it again and again.

And yet, strangely, mysteriously, as if my coworker had known something I didn't, I kept hearing this little voice in my mind telling me to be cautious, to concentrate, to focus. But on what?

Soon came the answer.

2

Texas Girl

I'M A TEXAS GIRL, THROUGH AND through. Grew up in and around Greenville, a town of 20,000, fifty miles northeast of Dallas and about that far from the Oklahoma border. Texas doesn't get much more Texas than Greenville, but of course you can say that about a lot of places in Texas. Texans sure do.

Like Houston and Austin, Greenville was named for a hero of the war of independence from Mexico, Thomas Green. It's located in what's called the Texas Blackland Prairies, which means oaklands and savannas as far as you can see. The largest employer in town was a defense contractor located at the small airport, which had been built secretly in World War II to train fighter pilots. When I was a kid, and maybe still, the company employed ten times as many people as the next biggest employer, the local school district. At one time, someone told me, about a fifth of the city worked for the company.

Greenville is hot and humid, and though I didn't realize it till I was much older, there's pretty much nothing to do. (Come to think of it, I didn't know it was hot and humid either, because I had nothing to compare it to. I assumed that that was normal weather for everyone.)

My first memory of being alive is lying in my crib and watching the sheer curtain billow above me, feeling the sunlight on my face. I really do remember that. The memory fits with what my mom said about me, that I was such an easy baby, she could put me down and walk away to tend to her chores without worrying.

This was in contrast to my brother Cory, two years older, who was always getting into trouble—and was often the chore Mom had to walk away and tend to when she left me in the crib. I'd feel guilty for having invaded his turf if Cory had been an easy child before I got there, but my mother said he never had been, from day one, so it wasn't only jealousy that turned him into a handful and a half. Mom used to sit him down beside me and feed both of us with bottles, one in each hand. This was well within her capabilities, coming from a family of powerful, determined women.

The affectionate term I called Mom's grandmother—my great-grandmother—was "Big Granny," and I came to consider her my guardian angel. Actually, I still do. An, enlarged, framed photo of her hangs on my bedroom wall, so it's her face I see every day when I wake.

Big Granny's name was Bertha Hollis, and even after her husband Jack died (before I was born), she lived on a farm that we'd visit on Sundays. It was about thirty miles north of Greenville, near the Sulphur River and the Ladonia Fossil Park, a huge preserve whose name describes exactly what it is (fossils from the Cretaceous and Pleistocene Periods). In winter the temperature would drop low enough for the house pipes to freeze over, meaning we'd have to use the outhouse to relieve ourselves. In the hot months, the adults would lock themselves in the one room with air conditioning and close the door to keep the cool in and the bugs out. (To this day, I still freak out about doors being open when the air conditioning is on.)

We kids—my brother and I and our cousins—were given a jug of water and told to stay outside all day, playing whatever came to mind. "Y'all have fun," she'd say. We swam in the horse troughs and teased the bull, seeing which of us could climb over the fence and get closest without being gored or trampled. We all got good at lifting up barbed wire without cutting ourselves to shreds or getting tetanus. And sometimes we hung out in the barn or played in the chicken coop, but that mostly smelled too bad.

The men—my dad and uncles and grandfather—would go out and shoot our Sunday dinner, usually rabbit, then cut off the feet and ask which of us wanted the lucky charm. Meanwhile the women—my mom and aunts and grandmothers—would sit and shell peas and peel tomatoes for the rabbit stew. If we decided on chicken instead, Big Granny would go into the coop, select the one she wanted, and swing it by its neck on the way back into the house.

A few times it was only Dad who'd go out, and he'd take me with him. We'd wade through the creek that ran through the property while he kept an eye out for water moccasins. When he saw them he'd blast them with his .22 rifle, never missing. My hero. In some places it was too deep for me, so he'd hoist me on his shoulders, where I'd keep a lookout for the snakes and tell him where they were. My hero. In the places where it was shallow, the water could get so hot in the summer that you felt like you were parboiling. He'd carry me there too. My hero.

Every time we left her, Big Granny would stand on the front porch and wave goodbye with tears in her eyes, even though she knew we'd all be back the following Sunday.

She'd had six kids, but one of them, a boy, had died of an ear infection in the era before antibiotics. The third of the five, and the only one still with us, is my grandmother Lois—Lois

Crofford, born July 1927. I consider her the fount of all
wisdom and common sense. Even as a little girl I believed she
knew things no one else knew and could see things no one
else could see. It is no exaggeration to say that she's responsible for, or has had a hand in, every major decision of my
life—or at least the ones that turned out well. Never have
I regretted taking her advice, but often have I regretted *not*
taking it. To this day, she lives alone in a large, two-story
house with a wraparound porch in a pecan grove, and takes
care of the whole place by herself, including picking pecans.
She's a strong woman, mentally and physically, and I flatter
myself by thinking we're alike.

3

Shredded

HEADING WEST AT ABOUT TWENTY-FIVE MILES an hour on my motorcycle along Ventura Boulevard in Woodland Hills, I stopped at a red light and was first at the line, with only a couple of cars behind me. When the light turned green, I had the right lane to myself and was going about twenty miles an hour when I noticed that, ahead of me about forty yards, an SUV was stopped at the end of a car dealership's driveway, waiting to turn into traffic. Its driver, a middle-aged man, and I exchanged eye contact, so I felt assured of my safety knowing he saw me. I assumed he planned to do what he was legally and logically supposed to do: wait for me, and the cars behind me, to pass before pulling out.

But that's not what happened.

He punched the gas just as I reached the driveway. (See what I mean about one second either way making a difference here?)

I saw him in my peripheral vision, and in a millisecond understood what was going on and recognized there was absolutely nothing I could do—no evasive action possible—to avoid being rammed by this big Ford Flex. If I didn't know better, I'd say he was actually trying to hit me. Anyway, it was a difference without distinction.

The noise of the impact sticks in my memory as something between a bomb and a bullet, but it's the pain that's most stuck with me because—well, it's still with me.

Having given birth twice, I can best describe the immediate, searing, piercing agony as what you imagine real torture victims endure at the hands of professional sadists—though I imagine knowing someone is intentionally trying to inflict maximum pain on you adds a whole new level of suffering. This was enough.

A witness later told me I looked as if I'd been catapulted into the air. I only remember sliding down Ventura Boulevard on the asphalt as if I were on a grinding stone, thinking, *Please don't let another car hit me.* I heard no brakes screeching, no bystanders scream, no horns honking—all of which, I later learned, actually had filled the air.

When I at last came to a stop I instinctively tucked into a fetal position to protect myself from being hit again. No one rushed to me. I lie there alone and noticed people walking slowly, apprehensively, no doubt wondering whether they should venture out into this mess. And then I glanced at my leg and realized their hesitancy, not to mention their faces frozen in horror, had to do with how bad off I looked.

Every beat of my heart issued a geyser of blood from what was a ruptured femoral artery in the middle of tissue damage that looked like a mangled mess of tissue. I grabbed for what was left of my leg and tried to keep the pieces from falling off and the blood from gushing. As much as it hurt, and as horrifying as it was, I found myself looking at it as if from afar, trying to decide how to describe it while I was looking at it. My right foot, for example, attached only by skin and my torn black leggings, dangled from the shin like a broken flower head.

Somewhere between five seconds and five minutes passed before I yelled out, "F---! Someone call 9-1-1!" and then,

"And call my husband!" followed by his cell phone number. My proper Methodist mother came to mind and I suddenly felt guilty for cussing, which led me to think about my job. *Oh, I guess I'm going to have to train my clients on crutches for a while,* which was a truly insane thought. Crutches? Anyone could see that I'd be lucky to keep my leg. And luckier still to survive. Yet I wasn't done with the insanity. I actually wondered whether Johnny would be pissed that a pulled pork sandwich had messed up his new backpack— his new backpack that, as I realized later, had actually saved my life because it was on my back that I'd slid after being hit. Without it, the grinding on the asphalt for that long a distance would've shredded my jacket and probably my skin and tissue right down to the spine. It's not for nothing that serious cycle riders wear outfits of leather.

I'm not sure if it was ten seconds or ten minutes before an honest-to-goodness good Samaritan came over to me, slipped off his belt, and fashioned it into a tourniquet around my leg. That simple act stopped the artery from spurting, and I'm not sure I even thanked him. He was like the Lone Ranger— just did his thing and left without knowing that, to this day, I think of him as a guardian angel.

Soon a middle-aged lady approached me and in a calm voice identified herself as a nurse. She clasped my hands and asked me to focus on breathing normally. She did it herself as an example, breathing in through her nose, and slowly out her mouth, knowing I'd automatically emulate her. But what made a much more powerful impression on me was her touch— holding my hands. I felt so grateful for that, especially because the driver who'd hit me just stood there, about eight feet away, arms across his chest, his face void of visible emotion, no doubt upset that he wouldn't soon be wherever he was in such a hurry to get to that he couldn't wait an extra five seconds.

The front bumper of his car had been sheared off by the impact.

With.

My.

Leg.

A crowd had begun to gather. One woman wandered over for a better view and got more than she'd bargained for. Fortunately, she didn't fall over like a tree when she fainted, which might have cracked her head; she simply crumpled the way dainty ladies do in movies.

I heard sirens and wondered whether they were for me. They were. Two ambulances, a fire truck, and an LAPD cruiser pulled up at about the same time. Johnny, who'd been waiting for me at home, came in right behind them in his truck. I'd shouted out his phone number so many times, a bunch of the bystanders had called him. Not recognizing the names or numbers in his caller ID, he'd let the first several calls go to voicemail, wondering what the hell was happening, before realizing that something serious must be up. By now, the cops had shut down Ventura Boulevard. Johnny pushed through the crowd that had gathered around me.

The look on his face is etched in my memory. It was a heart-breaking mix of horror, sadness, and panic.

But at least he was looking at me. The paramedics showed no emotion, which I understood, but they wouldn't make eye contact, which I didn't understand. Or did I? Was I assuming correctly that my condition was far worse than even the excruciating pain indicated? Were they trying to avoid a human-to-human connection with someone they thought would soon be dead?

With practiced skill, the paramedics got me onto a board, immobilized my head and neck, and strapped me down. The pain was indescribable, meaning I can't possibly find the words to describe it other than to say that on a 0-10 pain scale, this was 659. I have passed a kidney stone and given birth twice, and I'd have put those at no more than an eight on the pain scale. Even if I hadn't been gritting my teeth and moaning, the paramedics would've known by the looks of things what I was enduring. One EMT filled the IV drip.

Another said he'd have to cut off my jacket. Being strapped down on the board already, I wouldn't be able to wriggle out of it. But I begged him to let me try.

"It's new," I said.

He was nice enough not to explain how my skidding along the street had already ripped it to shreds. Then he helped me, probably thinking I was a lunatic. Or maybe not. Maybe he'd seen people dozens of times in horrible accidents focusing on ordinary minutiae as either a reaction to the trauma or to avoid contemplating the extent of the damage. Because at that very moment, assessing the situation, there couldn't have been a single one of those EMTs who doubted I'd soon be minus a leg. If I survived.

Before the paramedic with the IV put it in my arm, I asked what was in it.

"Morphine," he answered.

I said, "I'm allergic to morphine. I had it once before and nearly died."

That was before Ruby's birth. She had proven to be stubborn like me even in the womb and was stuck breach, so I had to have a Cesarean. I'd given birth the first time, to Savanna, with no drugs or intervention, and was intent on doing it again for Ruby. But the doctor convinced me to consider the health of my baby even if I didn't worry about my own. The anesthesiologist had administered morphine before the cut. Almost immediately I couldn't breathe. My heart was slowing to a halt from what they soon determined was anaphylactic shock that they cured with epinephrine. So while it ended up working out all right, in this situation I didn't have to worry about the health of my baby, only my own.

"I'm sorry," the paramedic said, "morphine is all we have. It's either morphine or nothing."

"I'll take the pain," I said. "I'd rather hurt than be dead."

In the fifteen minutes it took to reach the hospital, bouncing over pitted, potholed streets, I often reconsidered my decision. Maybe death was better than this. But no. There was Ruby to think about, and Savanna, and of course Johnny. To this day I feel bad for the paramedic sitting closest to me. Throughout the ride, I squeezed his leg as hard as I could—and I can squeeze hard—in reaction to the pain. Poor guy. Many a man has regretted trying to show off in the weight room only to learn in humiliating fashion that I'm a lot stronger than he is.

At last we arrived at Northridge Medical Center. A gurney appeared. And as they lifted me onto it for transport inside, I asked if someone could retrieve my jacket.

"Wow," the paramedic said, "you sure love that thing."

"I do."

But after all that, I never saw it again.

4

Survival Mechanisms

AS AFFECTIONATE AS MOM WAS, DAD was just as stand-offish. That had to do both with his temperament and his severe allergies. I'm really not sure how he did his job as the owner of a successful sign-painting company that put up everything from frontage signs on businesses to billboards. Creative Sign was the call nearly every business, from medium to large—even to huge, like the defense contractor in our area—in a wide geographical area made if a sign or billboard was needed. How did he do it? Keeping up the brand entailed shaking hands, attending meetings, offering bids, making sure customers got to see Biff Brown himself, being on-site when conditions were less-than-sanitary—all that stuff.

If one of us kids was going to sneeze, he'd pull his shirt up over his face and shut his eyes, then run and wash up. When I was thirteen, my school picked me to participate in the prestigious "Olympics of the Mind" extracurricular project for outstanding students. It required passing an audition, then writing, producing, and acting in a skit, followed by building a structure out of balsa wood and covering it in *papier-maché*. At the time, my parents had recently separated and were living in different houses, so when my team and I won the statewide competition, I excitedly asked Mom to drop me off at Dad's house with the project, expecting him to show how proud he was of me.

"Dad!" I shouted, "We got first; we got first!"

Instead of hugging me or even pretending to be excited, he flinched at the sight, covered his face, and said, "Get that thing away from me." He thought the newspaper, flour, and water that comprised the *papier-maché* were laced with dangerous mold.

This thing I'd conceived of and created had been judged the best in the state was less important to him than the fear he might get sick. Yes, he could've said, "That's great, you won. Now could you put that over there?" Instead, he snuffed out my enthusiasm.

What's telling, and even strange, is that I didn't feel trashed or even personally snuffed out. Maybe because I'd sadly already had so much practice at stuff like this, I made myself understand that with the kind of allergies he suffered, he needed to be cautious. And besides, what made me think I'd be entitled to a hug this time? How foolish I'd been to expect the impossible. That's the kind of kid I was, always rationalizing.

It was a kind of survival mechanism learned early on, even before that day I came home at age eight to hear the bad news. Dad sat Cory and me down, with my two-year-old little brother Micah roaming around, to explain he and Mom were separating and would now be living apart. Permanently.

Cory began laughing, thinking Dad was doing his jokester thing—not that anyone would ever joke to their kids about something like this, but at ten Cory couldn't have known that.

Me, I understood why he thought this was a joke. Never had Dad and Mom fought in front of us, or even exchanged harsh words. Yet for some reason, as upset as I felt, part of me wasn't surprised. Cory, obviously, was. Or so it seemed. I don't know. We didn't talk about it, same as we didn't talk about anything. Me, I saw things. I observed. I listened to what wasn't being said or done as much as what wasn't being said or done.

That didn't mean, however, I didn't feel like the world had shifted on its axis, or that I'd have to learn whatever the new laws of physics were. If it's true there are three sides to every dispute like this—her side, his side, and reality—there was no way to know which was which. And why would it matter anyway? Nothing was going to change the situation.

A few days later my grandmother took me out for a walk and tried to console me, explaining that sometimes men and women who are husband and wife, even if they're mother and father, have problems. *Et cetera.* I felt consoled for about fifteen seconds, then went on with my life, recognizing that shouting at the rain won't make it stop.

Sometimes things just don't work out for couples. It's only other people who need to find a reason for what happened, as if the marriage were a physics experiment.

5

Strong for Me

AS SOON AS THE EMT ROLLED me into the hospital on a gurney, I became aware of the commotion surrounding me. And not only from doctors and other medical personnel. There were so many cops there, I thought an officer had been shot on duty. But it turned out they were there for me.

What I learned is that, when you're married to a cop, you're in the extended family, and the law-enforcement extended family is the biggest family in the world. Like bad news, word had spread faster than the ambulance could get me there.

Though several doctors were tending to me, my attention was drawn to an awful sound—the keening of a man crying. I'd never before heard a man cry that hard, that painfully, that pitifully, and in my stupor and confusion and agony I couldn't imagine what had happened until I saw the man: my husband Johnny. He was pacing quickly, like a pinball, in a short radius, aware of what I wouldn't know for several days. The doctors were trying to reattach my femoral artery, and if they couldn't, I'd lose my leg immediately in the hope of saving my life. At this point, the doctor was trying to wrangle the artery like a greased pig. It kept popping back out of my leg and, for that matter, his hands.

I'd still been given nothing for the pain, and my head was still taped to the to board on the gurney, preventing me from curling myself into a fetal ball as instinctive protection against the hurt. But right now what bothered me most was Johnny's wailing. He couldn't control himself, this man who as a Highway Patrolman had been first on the scene, two years before, of a horrific head-on collision in Chatsworth, California, between a Union Pacific freight train and a commuter train caused by the commuter train's engineer running a signal because he'd been texting. The damage was horrific—twenty-five dead on the scene and dozens more badly injured. Johnny was pulling out dead bodies, some of them headless, and carrying the injured and screaming out of harm's way, all with absolute professionalism and detachment. Yet here he was, a helpless puddle of emotion that I could hear above the cacophony of other chattering voices and noises in the room."

"Johnny!" I shouted, "I need you to get over here right now and be strong for me!"

And just like that old E. F. Hutton commercial whose tagline was, "When E. F. Hutton talks, people listen," people listened.

The room went from chaos to silent, and I took comfort knowing that whatever happened to me, Johnny would be able to hold it together. I reached out my hand, he gripped it, and I held onto him, both hands, squeezing so hard I'm surprised he didn't wince himself. Apparently, my shout was the equivalent of those slaps you see in movies that snap people out of their hysterical reactions.

One of the nurses came over, a truly beautiful young woman, and leaned close to my face. Touching my cheek, she said, "We're going to give you something to make you feel better now."

I looked up at her, moved by the kindness in her voice, and almost cried, vowing silently to one day let this woman know how grateful I was to her—and when that day came, months later, she told me, "You know, as soon as you said what you did to your husband, and the way you said it, how you yelled like that, we all knew instantly the kind of person we were dealing with."

At the time, all I could think of was how I'd been wanting to ride my cycle that day in order to prove something that needed no proof: that I'd recovered completely from the first accident. But that's all of life—isn't it?—making decisions for whatever reason, not knowing what the future holds. The door you entered versus the one you didn't. The road not traveled versus the one you took.

To this day, I don't know what was injected into me. I know only that it put me out. Being awake and in agony would've been a hindrance to the doctors and nurses trying to help me, with no benefit to myself. If it's a choice between treating a compliant, unconscious patient and a demanding one who's in agony, which would you choose if you were a doctor?

Not that they had a choice anyway. As I later learned, my organs were shutting down from my being in shock due to trauma and loss of blood, so the only way to treat me was to put me out, out, out.

6

Cowgirl Up

IN SPRING 2016, A STORY THAT briefly made national news struck a chord with me. Some tourists visiting Yellowstone National Park saw a bison calf which appeared to have been abandoned by his mother or the herd. Standing by the road in a beautiful valley (well, all of Yellowstone is beautiful), it was crying out in anguish—lonely, afraid, and probably hungry. Others had seen the calf in the previous couple of days, since whatever accident or phenomenon had left him alone. But these tourists took pity on the calf and lifted it into their SUV for a trip to the ranger station. They figured they were doing something good, something humanitarian. They assumed that the rangers would know how to nurse the little fella to adulthood, then release him back into the wild.

But they were soon disabused of that notion, and were very nearly fined for interrupting nature's course. The rangers confirmed that the calf had indeed been abandoned and then euthanized it—doing more humanely what would've happened in a matter of days, even hours: it would have died as some other predator's meal (coyote, wolf, bear). Bison cows do not adopt another cow's offspring, and while occasionally a bull may agree to let a wayward calf tag along, the calf will not have learned what it's supposed to learn from Mom, and its life will be short, nasty, and probably painful and hungry.

Nature is vicious. Nature is heartless. Nature is indifferent to suffering—or, for that matter, to pleasure. Darwin's observation about the survival of the fittest describes nature as succinctly as it can be described. And, as it happens, that description extends also to people, we who have the self-awareness to comprehend our surroundings and situation, and take steps necessary to get out of danger or improve our lives. But ironically, it's that self-awareness that sometimes sabotages us and our best interests. Let me explain by asking you to think of your best, favorite dog ever.

When a dog is sick or old or even dying, it tries to carry on as best as it can without stopping to consider what it's lost. So if your Labrador is suffering from, say, hip dysplasia and has to limp, or can't get up/down the stairs or jump up on the couch the way it used to in the good old days, it accepts reality and does only the things it can—even if it has to remind itself, by trying and failing, that it can't do those things anymore. What the dog doesn't do is mope and feel sorry for itself. It has no self-pity.

People, of course, feel sorry for ourselves that we may be losing our best friend, or wish our best friend could still go to the park and catch Frisbees. But the dog itself isn't burdened by lamenting the past and fearing the future. To the degree it can, it puts one foot in front of the other—and we admire that. In fact, that's often what we admire most about our dogs, that they're in the here and now, always trying to make the most of the moment.

Life can be cruel. Life can be hard. Reality can be heartless, and in some ways, we share a fate with that bison calf and every beloved dog. But, like them, it's in our own best interests not to sabotage ourselves with self-pity, the kind that keeps us wondering about *why* instead of focusing on *why not.*

I learned from an early age to follow my mother's advice and "suck it up." Of course, at the time, there was no alternative to doing that. "Suck it up" or "cowgirl up" was Mom's way of imparting to me the lessons that poor little bison calf didn't get a chance to learn, and even Dad, in his own way—unintentional though it many have been—was educating me to the ways of world. Stopping to wonder why reality wasn't prettier wouldn't have done a thing for me. It would have crippled me then, preventing me from achieving everything I wanted to achieve, and crippled me years later when I was actually crippled, preventing me from choosing to accept nothing less than recovery.

As it happened, Mom and Dad weren't the only teachers from whom I absorbed realistic lessons.

7

Yeah Texas, You Still Have Your Leg

"SHE'S OPENING HER EYES. SHE'S OPENING her eyes."
The nurse's voice was the first thing I heard when I woke from my deep sleep to a living nightmare. Tubes in my arms and legs connected me to machines, and one was down my throat, delivering air straight to my lungs.

Strangely, as if I hadn't been asleep at all, I knew exactly where I was, I knew I was at the hospital in Northridge. I remembered the motorcycle accident, figured out pretty quickly that I was in a bed in the intensive-care unit, and wondered whether I still had a leg. But with my neck still immobilized, I couldn't look down to see. Johnny could see me trying.

"Yeah, Texas, you still have your leg," he said. He was leaning over me, tears in his eyes, looking drained.

For whatever reason, probably all the drugs, at that moment I didn't feel any pain in my leg. But without thinking what might happen, I instinctively tried to pull the breathing tubes out.

"No, no, no," one of the nurses said. "Don't pull them out. Don't do that, dear."

Good thing people were there to stop me. They grabbed my arms.

But I needed to tell Johnny something. Something urgent. Being intubated, though, I could only make sounds.

"She's trying to talk," the nurse said. "Get her a pad and a pen."

Someone did. I wrote as fast as I could, "Get off my tubes!" and showed it to Johnny, who was leaning over me, pressing on the tubes connected to the respirator, cutting off my air. I don't know how I figured that out.

He stepped back, and I'd like to say we all laughed about the fact that, for my first message, I hadn't written "I love you" or something to the effect of, "Where am I? What happened?"

But we didn't because there wasn't anything funny about this and I'd already begun writing a second note: "Don't tell Savanna." My older daughter, who was in eighth grade at the time, was on her East Coast trip looking at colleges. I didn't want her to worry. But I still hadn't been told how long I was out. Or how serious my condition was. Turns out, she'd been back for days. And she already knew about the accident.

I'd been out cold for seven days. They'd had to spread Vaseline over my eyes and lips to keep them from drying out. That explained why Johnny looked so exhausted. He'd been there every day, for at least half the day if not the whole day, alternating with my mother, who'd flown in from Texas. One would sleep in a chair beside me at night while the other stayed at home with Ruby. Odd as it sounds, not till I saw Mom did it strike me how serious this was. *Wow, if she took off work to come all the way out here, this must be bad.*

8

It Hurts to be Pretty

I WAS A BORN TOMBOY, AND it drove my mother crazy. She wanted me to wear dresses and frilly things. When I was eight she even enrolled me in a beauty pageant. Those pageants are a big deal in Texas, especially for the little girls who want to be in them so people will think they're pretty. It's also a big deal for their mothers. Me, I would've rather had the stomach flu than stand up there on that stage in a pink taffeta dress, patent leather shoes, and panty hose—panty hose!—pretending not to be embarrassed and pretending to act as if I thought I deserved to be there. It's not with undue modesty that I say I was ugly at that age. I was a skinny little girl with big buck teeth and short curly hair that Mom tried always to blow out straight, not knowing what else to do with it. Every time she pulled the brush through, it hurt my tender scalp, but she kept on even when the brush snagged and I'd wince and whimper. "It hurts to be pretty," she'd say, which was the companion to "Hide your crazy and be a lady." Translation: Put a lid on it; suck it up; don't let see anyone see anything other than a Southern belle.

Poor Mom. Being girly didn't come naturally to me, and I think it pretty much drove her crazy, wondering if I was ever going to get there. Even as I made it to my teen years,

I wore no makeup, dressed in my brother's hand-me down 501s, a white t-shirt, combat boots, and khaki army jackets I'd bought at the Army-Navy surplus store. Old flight jackets too. To this day I'm not sure we put braces on my teeth because I needed them and she worked for an orthodontist, or because she thought once my teeth were straight, I'd start acting like a girl.

I know for a fact, though, that when I was three she enrolled me in a dance class at a studio in town she'd heard about not because she knew I loved to dance but because it was the girlie thing to do.

Oh, well. Whatever her motivation, it was one of the best things she ever did for me. God does work, after all, in mysterious ways.

9

Wrangling a Greased Pig

IT WOULD BE A WHILE TILL Johnny told me the whole story of how, after the coma was induced, the vascular surgeon had rushed into the emergency room—and I'd caught my first break. (In retrospect, I consider this my second break. The first break would be having had Johnny's backpack on, the one that kept me from being shredded down to the bone on the street.)

Normally on three-day weekends, any of the specialty surgeons on-call or already on duty are low man/woman on the totem pole, often with professional skills to match their standing. But not this time. Luckily, Dr. Adel Jabour, a first-class vascular surgeon, came running in. He was wearing a suit before taking off the coat and putting on a protective apron while gloving up. Someone apprised him of what happened, but he could see for himself I was in danger of bleeding out through my femoral artery.

Dr. Jabour reached into my leg and felt around, trying to find the artery, grab it, and lift, which apparently is only somewhat easier than wrangling a greased pig. "I got it!" he yelled before Johnny heard a snap, like a rubber band, then, "Damn, lost it."

After another couple of tries, Dr. Jabour held up the

artery and clamped it. Which saved my life for the moment. But could my leg be saved? The answer wouldn't be known till he performed surgery, taking an unused artery from the other leg and transplanting it into my bad leg—in essence, replacing the damaged femoral artery.

The operation took almost three hours. Johnny was down in the cafeteria with two of his CHP buddies—the hospital still crawling with them, thanks to the brotherhood of law enforcement officers—when Dr. Jabour came in to tell him the operation had gone as well as could be expected but they wouldn't know for forty-eight hours if the artery was going to take and supply my leg properly with blood. If not, it would have to be amputated.

"Okay," Johnny said, "forty-eight hours. But how will you know?"

The doctor explained that the big toe has a pulse that would be monitored every hour for at least the next forty-eight.

"But right now," the doctor said, "things look good."

Johnny relaxed for the first time in hours, he told me later, and that allowed the tears to flow out from a combination of relief and anxiety.

Then the orthopedic surgeon on call came in and introduced himself to Johnny. He said, "Mr. Lago, short of a battlefield wound, like an IED, I've never seen a bone injury this bad."

All the bones below my knee—tibia, fibula, foot—weren't much more intact than confetti. I'd had something called a plateau fracture, meaning the head of the tibia where it connects to the knee was broken in half, preventing it from operating as a ball socket. That's why it wouldn't bend.

"We need to amputate," the doctor said.

"Excuse me?"

"That is the only way to save her life."

"Dr. Jabour just told me we have forty-eight hours to see if the artery is delivering enough blood."

"We should amputate. And we have to move soon. I need your consent."

"No disrespect, doctor," Johnny said, "but no."

Though panicked now, Johnny still managed to think straight. That's what years of being at accident scenes had taught him, and, as it happened, he immediately called someone whose life he'd saved in a motorcycle accident a few years before: Dr. Henry Lubow, head of the trauma unit at UCLA.

Lubow took his call and asked, "Who's your ortho?"

Johnny told him.

"Oh, no," Lubow said. He recognized the name and knew the man's reputation. "Don't let him touch her."

Henry instructed Johnny to get a cease and desist order, preventing the hospital from taking any further action without his express consent. So while Johnny still had the phone to his ear, he walked over to the office where the doctor in charge of that shift on the ICU happened to be. Johnny told her what he wanted. Seeing that he was being instructed by someone on the phone, she asked who was advising him. He said a close personal friend and gave Henry's name. She knew who Henry was and asked if she could speak to him. Johnny handed her the phone, and listened to one side of the conversation as they worked out that Henry would somehow now be considered the attending physician.

Word soon reached the orthopedic surgeon that he'd been yanked off the case and couldn't do anything more than check on what was called the *external fixator* that he'd installed during the emergency operation. It's a type of medical device that is either clamped onto or screwed into bones and tissue that need stabilizing; *contraption* is probably a more descriptive word than device. The doctor stormed over to where Johnny was and told him he was making a terrible mistake.

Johnny ignored him and began Googling "limb salvage," a term he'd learned over the years from the number of horrific accidents he'd seen as a CHP officer. He'd often have to check a deceased person's license for that little dot indicating that the holder had agreed to be an organ donor, then communicate with the coroner's office, which presumably would speed their personnel to maintain the integrity of the deceased's organs. And while we hadn't yet gotten to the point where arms and legs could be transplanted onto stranger's bodies, in cases where limbs had been severed from still-living accident victims, "limb salvage" was the term medical personnel on-site used for the art of reattaching limbs. While not always certain, the science was far from fiction.

From what Johnny could see, the best limb-salvage physician in Southern California, maybe the country, was Dr. Donald Wiss, who worked out of Cedars-Sinai, in West Hollywood, about thirty miles away. It's generally acknowledged that Cedars is the best hospital in the area, and one of the best in the country. The problem was getting in to see a guy like Wiss. This was Los Angeles, where some doctors have celebrity cred, and may be as difficult to get near. No doubt, Dr. Wiss fell into that category. You can't pick up the phone and expect to get an appointment, especially in an emergency situation. You need an invitation, or at least a referral. It's kind of like the difference between waiting in the rope line at a nightclub, and being ushered through the VIP entrance.

As it happened, Henry Lubow happened to be one of those A-list docs who can get the A-lists docs on the phone— or at least offer an opinion about them. And by divine coincidence, just as Johnny completed his Google search, Henry walked into the hospital to see his newest patient—me.

"Wiss?" Henry said. "That's my guy. That's who put me back together after my accident."

"Look, Doc," Johnny said. "You have to call him for me."

"I will," Henry said.

He did.

Two hours later Johnny's phone rang. "Mr. Lago?" said the voice. "This is Donald Wiss. I'm out of town at a lecture right now, but I have a team ready for your wife as soon as she's stabilized."

It was set. Johnny, I later heard, broke down and cried out of accumulated grief, fear, and tension. Finally, something good was happening.

10

Dancing, Dancing

FOR AS LONG AS I CAN remember, I needed to be constantly moving. I'm sure I was dancing before I knew what dancing was—that is, moving my feet rhythmically, jumping around, being in action—but by age three I was *dancing* dancing. And I never didn't want to be dancing. Imagine how tiring that is to be around.

"Be still," Mom would tell me about fifty times a day, and, "Get out of the kitchen if you're gonna be doing that," about sixty times a day—"that" being shuffling, dancing, pirouetting, jumping, tapping, and every other form I'd learned.

Even when I was in dance class, in between lessons I would continue moving my legs, so sometimes my dance teachers would tell me to be still. It's a good thing I grew up when I did and where I did. Nowadays they think every kid with energy to burn, especially boys, must have some form of ADHD that requires medication.

The school did, though, put me in the class for slow learners after teachers observed me shuffling my feet and looking around the room, and for essentially making up my own form of writing and creating my own lessons. Not till the eighth grade did the school test me and discover—ta-da!—I was gifted. What they'd interpreted as slow was actually me being ahead of the class and exhibiting symptoms of boredom. If something didn't challenge me, I lost interest and focus.

Dancing challenged me. Dancing interested me.

Given how I loved dancing and how quickly I could pick up the steps taught to me, you'd think I had athletic tendencies. But I sucked at any sport played with a ball. Logically, I should attribute that to poor hand-eye coordination, except for the fact that I couldn't play soccer either—played with the same feet I danced with. The coach kicked me off the church basketball team—the church team!—after one game. And I was so bad at tennis, the coach made me water girl, which was good in another way because all I had to do was deliver the water to the court and then I was on my own, so I got to leave school forty-five minutes early and go teach dance.

It's not that I didn't try to play these sports. I did. All of them. This was Texas, where sports are king, queen, and prince. But for whatever reason, I wasn't interested.

11

Connections

THE FOLLOWING FEW NIGHTS IN THE hospital, Johnny wound up in long conversations with Dr. Jabour—usually, he said, in the wee hours of the morning, when Jabour would show up to check on the pulse in my leg and drink coffee with Johnny. The two had taken a liking to each other, and not only because of Johnny's gratitude for what the doctor had done to save my life, and then—so far, at least—my leg. There was also Jabour's law enforcement background. He was a reserve officer in a local police department; a sergeant. They talked about all sorts of things, and on the night he delivered the news that it appeared the femoral-artery transplant he'd done would save my leg, he asked where Johnny was transferring me.

"Cedars," Johnny answered.

"Who's your doctor there?"

"Wiss," Johnny replied.

"Wiss—how'd you get him?" Dr. Jabour asked, surprised and impressed.

"Connections," Johnny said with a wink and a nudge.

Dr. Jabour said, "I heard about your confrontation with the orthopedic surgeon."

"He took it personally," Johnny said. "I think he just

wanted to amputate no matter what."

"Well, that may well be true," Jabour said. "But I have to tell you, John, there's going to be a lot of pain down the line. More than you can imagine. This may not be the best decision."

"Maybe not," Johnny said. "But, believe me, I've been in the hospital plenty of times, waiting to take statements, when somebody wakes up from an operation after an accident, sees a limb missing, and totally freaks out. It's a horrible thing. So I don't want this to be my decision. Whatever ends up happening, as long as there's a choice to be made, I want it to be Amberly's decision. When she makes it, then I'll know I've done my job. And whatever she decides is fine with me."

12

Number Seven

AT EIGHT, I DECIDED WHAT I wanted to do with my life.
I'd actually known what I wanted to do—that is, knew what
gave me incredible pleasure doing—since I was three. But I
didn't realize till I was eight that was how I wanted to earn
my keep as an adult.

I wanted to dance.

When I was three, the whole family (Micah wasn't born
yet) went to Dairy Queen one Friday night after the high
school football game, same as everyone else in town. It was
crowded in there, and hot. The place was buzzing. And for
whatever reason, on the impetuous spur of the moment, I
jumped up on the table and began dancing, fooling around,
making up steps as I went along to the beat of whatever music
piped through the jukebox. I don't know why my parents
didn't tell me to get down, or maybe they did and I ignored
them, but I kept at it pretty much until we left, entertaining
everybody—most of all myself.

After that I'd dance wherever I was, even while waiting
in line somewhere. I'd dance my way down the street because
walking didn't do it for me, dance while brushing my teeth,
and dance while getting dressed for school. It's hard to say

whether I had any talent for dancing, though at that age talent is a byproduct of passion, and passion I had by the bushel. Where it came from is a mystery, though when my daughter Ruby was only three she suddenly decided that all she ever wanted to do was ride horses. And so she has, her passion never waning, only growing along with her skills. So maybe these things really are genetic.

By five, and for the next few years, people would insist I be at the Dairy Queen after every Friday night football game, dancing on the table, everyone clapping rhythmically. The odd thing was I didn't do it for attention, and anyway it wasn't the attention I liked best. What I loved was the dancing itself. Yes, I was glad people enjoyed it and showed their enjoyment in a way I could appreciate. But that was less important to me than my own enjoyment. If ever I had stopped loving dancing, I wouldn't have stood up on those tables and performed, no matter how badly they may have begged me.

Then it happened. At eight, I put two and two together and realized that dancing was something you could do as an adult and get paid for, the way Dad got paid to put up signs and Mom got paid for being a secretary.

How did I know you could get paid for dancing? Television. That year, MTV went on the air. I watched it religiously, always on my feet, dancing to whatever song was playing, mimicking—if I could—the professional dancers who were such a big part of music videos back in those early days. That's when I decided that I would (a) someday be one of them, and (b) move to Los Angeles, where I'd been told that most of these videos were shot. How else could I be one of them if I wasn't there? Obviously, I'd have to wait a few years and hone my chops, but that excited me. Having a goal, a destination, was exactly what I needed. God knows I didn't want to stay in Greenville the rest of my life, and knowing I'd someday be getting out made every day easier because every day that passed was one day closer to my leaving—as long as I used that day to be better at the thing that was going to get me out of there.

Of course, to do that I couldn't be the cute little girl dancing on table tops; couldn't be the little girl who probably had talent but never developed it. I had to be a girl who worked for what she wanted to achieve. Don't ask me how I knew that either.

The dance studio in town where Mom enrolled me was called Academy of Dance Arts. It specialized in tap dancing and training girls to perform as a troupe. Girls who were good enough would be selected to participate in dance competitions regionally, then statewide and even nationally.

You might think tap was outmoded, and in some ways it was, this being before the time of Savion Glover but long after Astaire and Kelly. There was, though, a popular performer of the era named Gregory Hines who made tap look like the coolest thing in the world, something everyone would want to do. And you could see how the rhythm and timing, if not the moves themselves, would be the foundation of any kind of dance. I took to it immediately, practicing my steps every moment I could, even in school, quietly, while sitting at my desk, in my regular shoes, during lessons. It got so that I didn't even realize I was doing it.

The one thing about tap is that it's noisy. Sure, ballet dancers have to hear music, but they don't create a racket the way tap dancers do. Learning your child wants to be a tap dancer is not unlike when your kid says he wants to be a drummer. You either learn to accommodate the din or you take away the drumsticks and tap shoes. Eventually, Mom put down a plank of wood in the garage and insisted I practice only in there, and only with the door down. That was fine by me.

Every year Al Gilbert, an instructor from Los Angeles considered to be the king of tap, came to town to see whether our studio, and the girls studying at it, were capable of doing justice to the art of tap dancing. My first year, I was too young to understand the dynamics, but I could tell by the way our teachers reacted both before and during his visit that this was a big deal. "He's famous," one of them said. And he was coming all the way from Los Angeles to grace us with his presence in little Greenville, Texas, which even we thought of as the middle of nowhere.

Anyway, that's how it came off. And as the youngest dancer in the studio, having to keep up with—and be better than—girls two and three years older, I was so nervous when he showed up that I cried to my dance teacher, Jackie Nutting. She pulled me aside, and in doing so happened to touch my distended belly.

"Bless your heart, Amberly," she said, "you have to go to the bathroom." So I went. And good thing I did, too, because I would've gone right through my tutu when my turn came.

All of us stood in a horizontal line in front of him, each with a number from one to ten, or however many of us there were. He'd call out a number and ask the person assigned that number a question or questions that required both a verbal response and a short demonstration of the step he asked about.

Seeing I was the youngest, and how nervous I was, he kindly gave me the easiest possible question: "Number seven, what's a shuffle?"

His light question, and my nerves, shouldn't have been necessary. All things being equal, nothing he could've asked was beyond my knowledge; that's how hard I'd worked and studied for this, knowing the stakes—passing entitled you to earn a ribbon and certificate, both of which I wanted as much as I'd ever wanted anything. But I couldn't hold a thought in my head.

A shuffle? You don't even have to have been a tap dancer to know that a shuffle is the easiest, most basic step in tap dancing. It's a front brush followed by a back brush.

But I tanked even that, freezing like water at absolute zero. Out of the goodness of his heart, I'm sure, I was allowed to pass. But I knew I hadn't earned it, so in a sense what had happened was a blessing in disguise, because I became the studio's most dedicated little dancer.

Day and night I practiced, foregoing pretty much everything else in my life except school. I vowed to myself to conquer every level of his exam, no matter how difficult it was or how long it took. I did. And not only did I take and pass the exam, but I also volunteered afterward to become a teacher and teach every level of the exam to other girls. Doing that didn't alone allow me to participate on stage in competitions and at conventions. What it did was demonstrate my commitment, and that commitment was what made me good enough to eventually be selected with all those older girls to compete. And it also helped me pay for the school.

At our first competition, a regional held in Dallas, the ten of us who'd been selected won the whole enchilada and were filmed for the national video. Not that coming in second or fifth or 179th would have dampened my enthusiasm. But what surprised and astounded me was my reaction when they announced the winner: I began crying. *Why am I crying? Oh, because you're happy. Weird.*

This was the first time I'd cried since the bad thing had started happening with Mom's husband, and they were tears of joy. The experience caught me off guard, and I decided that from now on, I'd cry *only* tears of joy. Never again, I vowed, would I cry tears of shame, humiliation, or pain. It was a bad and stupid decision, but I needed to make it in order to make sense of things.

The bigger moral was that I'd tasted victory, believed it was possible, and wanted to keep tasting more.

13

They Want to Amputate

I LOOKED DOWN AT MY RIGHT leg, encased in bandages and that contraption I would later learn was called an external fixator, which I came to think of over the next couple of days as an instrument of torture. Right now I was surprised not to be hurting too much, but of course I had some of the heaviest pain medications known to science dripping into my veins.

Several medical people have since told me that bone pain is the worst kind, but that was something I learned the hard way.

Afterward was when Johnny came, clearly shaken by what he'd heard, and quietly related what had happened with the orthopedic surgeon.

"He wants to amputate," he said.

"No, no way," I said. "Uh-uh. Never. No. No. No. No. No."

14

Every Other Weekend

IN A LOT OF WAYS, TEXAS is a whole other country. Kids, at least when I was growing up, weren't pampered and protected by bubble wrap. This was certainly true of the way my mother approached child-rearing. For that matter, she wasn't afraid of corporal punishment, either, and believed that sparing the rod spoiled the child.

As a consequence, I don't remember a time in my life when I didn't feel mature. My parents, especially Dad, must have felt that way about me too. The terms of the divorce were that my brothers and I were to spend every other weekend at his house. But some of those weekends Dad was out of town. I realize that these days it would probably be considered child neglect, but when it was my brothers and me alone at Dad's for those fifty-four hours of the weekend, I didn't think twice about being left, at eight, to make sure two-year-old Micah and ten-year-old Cory ate properly. I cooked for them, same as I would have if Dad had been there. Matter of fact, I also cleaned his house and scrubbed his toilets. I don't know why I thought to do all this or considered it my responsibility.

Needless to say, none of us ever told Mom about that.

There was no reason to. And by then she'd moved on to her second husband and the two children they'd have together over the next four years.

15

Are We There Yet

WHEN WORD GOT OUT THAT I'D awakened, the ICU waiting room filled up with friends wanting to see me—bless them all. But most of them never got the chance because my mother guarded the door like a sentry, letting only a few people pass after they'd gowned up, because the risk of that open wound becoming infected was so extreme. Besides, I wasn't very good company for anyone who did get in. The pain made me cranky enough, the waiting made me even crankier, and the pain meds kept me in a daze, so even if I did speak for a few minutes with someone, I'd have no memory of it a few minutes later. Anything that wasn't directly related to my leg, and me getting out of the hospital, didn't stick.

"When am I getting out of there?" I kept asking, like a little kid in the back of the car: "Are we there yet?" Every moment I spent in Northridge was a wasted moment, a limbo moment—a moment I wouldn't be taking the first step on that journey of a thousand miles.

I do remember when Dr. Jabour came in. Johnny introduced me. I thanked him for what he'd done. Then he leaned in close so no one else could hear, and whispered, "I need to ask you something, just between and me."

"Okay."

"Do you have a problem with drug abuse?"

"What? No, sir. I have never taken a drug in my life. Not once. I don't even take aspirin." I was confused and wondered why he would even ask me that.

"Then, are you an athlete?"

"Yes. I've been an athlete all my life. I never miss a day of working out."

"That explains it then."

"Explains what?"

"We had to administer three, four, five times the normal amount of pain meds it should've taken because of all the endorphins in your system."

"Well, let me tell you," I said, "right before the accident that day I had come from running eleven miles in my fastest time ever." What I didn't mention was that the day before that, I'd been the star of a fitness video for a company called CoreFit, and I considered myself to be in the best shape of my life, which was saying something.

"So you were full of endorphins," he said. "No wonder."

He smiled, and wished me well, probably not believing I would ever get well—or even walk again on my own two feet—but he said, "You're going to save me a dance. We'll dance together."

I chose to believe him.

16
Maternal Love

UNTIL I WAS A LITTLE BIT older and began babysitting and tutoring and saying yes to any work offered me—including working at the dance studio—to earn my own money, my mom worked two jobs to put food on our table and to make sure I had the money to keep paying the studio for my lessons. First she'd worked as a secretary for an attorney, and on the side typed audio transcripts of doctors' notes, somehow getting that medical terminology down on the page flawlessly. Then she began working for an orthodontist, where she worked for years. In the realm of intellect, Mom is one very smart person.

She cared about nothing besides being a good mom, and she was old school. You didn't dare talk back to her. One time I did and got slapped. I still tease her about when she'd chase me around with a paddle, and how if, at a fair or birthday party, I ever won one of those little paddles with the rubber balls attached by a rubber band, I'd not bring it home, knowing it could someday be used as a weapon on my bottom. On the other hand, a paddle like that was better than the wooden spoon she used to whack me and my brothers with. These days someone would call child services. Back then, it was considered a certainty that if you spared the rod you'd raise a spoiled child. I didn't take offense to it, and though I have never and would never hit my own children, I accepted it then as a sign of maternal love—probably because I could see it didn't give Mom any pleasure; in fact, it pained her.

Neither Mom nor Dad ever tried to get me and brothers interested in anything—completely the opposite of so-called helicopter parents today who schedule their kids' lives down to the quarter hour with play dates and lessons and extracurricular activities. My parents, to the degree they thought about it, must have assumed we'd somehow discover whatever it was that turned us on, and if nothing did, then so be it. But Mom saw what dancing meant to me.

Cory seemed to have zero ambitions beyond sleeping late and beating the crap out of me, something he delighted in, especially when picking me up and throwing me against the wall. The way he laughed made me come back at him and try to get my licks in. But I didn't grow to five eleven till after high school. For most of childhood, I was a scrawny little thing, short and skinny, and he thought it was the funniest thing in the world to launch me against anything solid.

Yes, I learned to fight back and defend myself, but he was never not bigger, stronger, and nastier, and there's something really sad about it, because even today we hardly have a relationship. I remember coming home to Mom's one afternoon after school without my key, so I went around to the back. The garage was open, which led into his room. He was there and warned, "Don't come through here."

But I had no choice; it was my only way in. And he full-on, fist-closed, punched me, rearing back like a boxer and smashing me in the face. He hit me so hard, the blood poured out from my lips that were now impaled on my braces.

Seeing what he'd done, it was the only time I saw him

scared. I said, "I'm telling Mom."

"Please don't," he begged. "I'm sorry; I'm sorry."

As much as it hurt where he'd hit me, I enjoyed watching him act scared by the sight of blood. Blood meant he'd get in trouble if Mom knew. The interesting thing was that the braces were probably responsible for a lot of the blood, by cutting my lips, but the braces may have saved me some teeth by holding them in place.

I didn't tell Mom. What would've been the point?

Years later he told Mom he felt bad for the way he used to beat on me. I appreciated hearing that, even if it didn't come directly from him.

Once when he hit me, I went wild, trying to swing and hit him back but flailing like a maniac because he was so much bigger and could grab my head like a melon and hold me at bay.

In retrospect, I suppose, I should thank him for being the catalyst who got me into regular boxing, *muay thai* boxing, and the Israeli self-defense discipline called *krav maga*. I wanted and needed the confidence that comes with knowing you can physically defend yourself—exactly what I'd lacked as a child against him. It worked too. I learned, in time, that I carry myself differently than I did as a kid, and not only because I'm more mature.

(When Johnny and I first started dating, we were wrestling around and he said, "Okay, Miss Krav Maga, get out of this," and he jumped on top of me while I was on the floor. Now remember, Johnny's six four and two twenty, but I easily bucked him off. He went flying, and the look on his face was something I'll never forget. My only regret is not learning this earlier, when I could've used it on my brother. That might've been good for both of us—a confidence-builder for me, and a wake-up call for him.)

The happiest moments my brothers and I shared from

our childhoods were, ironically, right after the divorce, when Dad bought an RV (a fifth wheel, as Texans say) and took us on camping trips over long weekends to sites in Oklahoma. Anyway, they were my happiest moments with the family, the closest glimpse I got into the kind of childhood every kid wants. Thanks to Dad, we went hiking (and it was here I developed my love for the trails), fishing, canoeing, and built campfires, roasted hot dogs and marshmallows. We stayed up late telling scary stories and made scary videos with Dad's first-generation camcorder, the one that looked as big as a Panavision real-life movie camera, sneaking up on everybody at the campfire to record their reaction. It was a blast. And, like a blast, short-lived.

I can't say I regret turning Dad down several times in the next couple of years for these camping trips, because the weekend or the week or however long he wanted to go for would've conflicted with dance. But I do wish I had more happy memories beyond those camping trips and his teaching me to ride motorcycles. Missing dance rehearsals, even one of them, meant you couldn't be in the competitions, and I wanted to be in the competitions more than I wanted anything else in life.

It was rare that Mom and her new husband Chuck, and soon her new young children (daughter Taylor and son Jordan) went away on vacations. But when they did, they always invited me. And I always said no, even though I was living with them—not, primarily, because of dance; but primarily because I was living with them. Come to think of it, because I was living with them was primarily why I spent so much at the dance studio and at school running track.

17

Spit and Prayers

I WAS IN A RUSH TO get out of the hospital and see what Dr. Wiss could do. And I did, two days later.

It was a Sunday, nine days after the accident. We couldn't wait any longer because we needed to travel on a day and at a time when traffic was likely to be reasonably free-flowing, which in the Los Angeles metropolitan area is between two and four AM every day, also from 11:16 to 11:29 AM Monday through Saturday, and finally before 1 PM on Sunday. (I'm only slightly kidding. All right, actually I'm not kidding at all.)

And it's too bad we had to drive. Our mode of transport for the thirty miles was supposed to have been a helicopter. Through the law enforcement grapevine, the pilot of an LAPD helicopter heard about me and got a message to Johnny that the training mission he was supposed to be on at UCLA hospital could be done at Northridge instead. All we had to do within the pilot's ten-hour window was get Northridge to sign me out and Cedars-Sinai to acknowledge that there was a bed for me. But Northridge was reluctant for liability reasons that I never understood, and Cedars kept insisting there was no bed for me. So tick-tock, the hours passed. At last Johnny called Dr. Wiss directly and left a voice message. An hour later Wiss called him back to say the red tape had been cut, the bed was waiting, the liability transferred to Cedars. But by then we'd missed the helicopter window. So now I'd have to ride in an ambulance.

Because my leg was mere pieces of bone being held together with little more than medical spit and prayers, they'd decided that the ambulance's maximum speed could be no faster than thirty-five miles an hour—and that the route would have to be the one with the fewest potholes, which the driver was ordered to avoid. Or try to. So instead of a twelve-minute air ride; instead of a thirty-five-minute car ride by the shortest route, we needed seventy-minutes on a route from Northridge to West Hollywood that was so round-about, if Google Maps navigation had been switched on, that annoying voice would've kept repeating, "No, you idiot, not that way."

The ambulance was accompanied the entire way by an informal CHP escort: Johnny and some of his friends who volunteered to do this on their day off, no charge, no lights or sirens.

Dr. Wiss's team of I don't know how many people was waiting for me at Cedars and sprang into action upon my arrival, like a well-rehearsed military unit, everyone with a job to do that they did with practiced efficiency and skill. I don't remember much about that ambulance ride except it seemed to last forever. What I do remember vividly is that my screams of pain were unbearable for Johnny to hear as they transferred me from the gurney to my new hospital bed, and I was grateful for my friend Ian who filled in for Johnny and held my hand.

At last I was in my bed in the room that would be my home for much longer than I anticipated. Johnny, I know, felt some relief at last knowing I was finally taking the first step of my journey toward healing. This whole prior week, everything had been on him. Now I'd been delivered, and he was able to let down.

After the nurses hooked me up to the IVs and steadied my leg, I asked when Dr. Wiss would be seeing me. A nurse explained that he wasn't in the hospital that day but would be in to see me the following day. A while later, a man wearing a brown blazer came in. I noticed right away he wasn't dressed like a doctor. And there was a nametag ID clipped to his breast pocket: "Dr. D. Wiss."

I tried to control the tears from rolling down my face. I wanted him to know I was no sissy and was determined to keep my leg. It was a good try. I all but screamed out, "Dr. Wiss, you're the man who's going to save my leg!"

He replied, "Well, we'll see about that. The first thing we're going to do tomorrow morning is take you in and clean this all up. I don't like where they've put those pins. There's a big risk of infection." Osteomyelitis—bone infection—is a big deal because it's so difficult to treat effectively.

He reached for my hand to shake. I grabbed his with both of my hands, as if clinging for dear life, and he said he'd see me the next day. Conspicuously, he hadn't promised he could save my leg. For that matter, I'm not sure that he, like Dr. Jabour, believed saving my leg was necessarily in my best long-term interest. I suspect he thought he might be able to save it, but at great cost to me in terms of quality of life. Because of the damage, some of it irreparable, to every structure in my leg—including its nerves—an intact leg would likely entail a lifetime of pain. So I guess he envisioned the day might come when I would ask them to take my leg in order to relieve me of chronic agony.

18
Super Chicks

I REMEMBER WITH PARTICULAR VIVIDNESS A day when I was nine. Cleaning up my room, I came upon some t-shirts my two cousins and I had had made up at the mall when we were five. The shirts had iron-on transfers, so popular in those days, that read, "Super Chicks" and each of our names next to images of fuzzy chicks. Wearing them, we formed the Super Chicks Club, with me as the president and chief instigator, and held our meetings, such as they were, in Big Granny's chicken hutch. Not much happened at these so-called meetings other than declaring ourselves "Super Chicks" and gabbing about what we were going to do, and could do, and could imagine doing when we got older.

Now, only four years later, I looked at my Super Chicks t-shirt that said *Amberly* on the front and cried for what turned out to be the last time in a very long time, feeling like the little girl who'd worn this thing so proudly had already died.

That was the year the abuse started, right after Mom married Chuck.

One night he came in my room and forced himself on me. Afterward he told me not to tell anyone. He warned, "If you tell anyone, I will hurt your mother." I believed him. I didn't tell anyone. So it kept going on.

And it changed everything about me, I'm sure. Even at that young age I knew what he was doing was wrong, and I knew I had done nothing to deserve this. And yet that godawful, crippling, paralyzing shame I felt inside meant I must've been doing something wrong.

I had to somehow rationalize it. I had to make up stories to myself and explain that this man was a role model to me, so this must be how daddies teach their daughters about the real world and growing up. The shame was like a cesspool that kept getting deeper and darker and more toxic. Safe was something I would never feel again. How could I?

One night at the dinner table in the kitchen, as Mom washed dishes with her back to us, Chuck sat with his back to her, staring at me. And as Mom said whatever she was saying to us, assuming we were listening, he mouthed to me with that demonic look on his face, "Just wait till your mother leaves."

Until I was thirteen, I always wore baggy t-shirts and sweatshirts, not wanting my body outline to show, and I refused to invite friends over, not wanting them to be anywhere in his orbit. The man earned his living, to the degree he earned a living, as a private investigator. He knew the boundaries of things and how far he could skirt them, and he terrified me.

"Come sit on my lap," he'd say, slapping his knees in an avuncular way, and Mom never understood why I didn't want to. She thought I was being difficult, and I couldn't tell her *why* I was being difficult: to save her from harm.

It was no accident that I spent six nights a week at the studio, or began running on the school track team, becoming good enough—fueled by anger and grief and terror—to be a state champion at 1200 meters and make my coach think I was good enough to become an Olympian. Consciously, I hadn't taken them up for what exercise like that did do a young girl's body, because I'd never learned about the physiological effects of extreme exercise on a girl's body. But by running and dancing so hard, I kept my body fat down so low that I failed to develop. Not till seventeen did I begin menstruating and developing breasts.

Had this all been an accident, or had it been a gift from heaven? I wouldn't put the gift beyond the realm of possibilities. I'd become a total tomboy, as capable as any of the guys riding motorcycles or shooting or swimming or climbing. I'd become the girl guys asked to fix them up with her friends. Not till after high school did I grow as tall as I was lean. Not till seventeen, four years after the last time he touched me, did I have my first boyfriend.

In the years I lived in my mother's home, I'd come home at night, exhausted, wanting only to heat up in the microwave the dinner Mom had left for me, then do my homework so I could keep up my 4.0 average in school. But he'd sneak into the kitchen, and I could feel him behind, leering—in my mind, drooling.

I had long before realized the little bit of power I had over him was not to let him see me break down emotionally. Before, he had always smiled when I whimpered, a grim, perverted, repellent, nauseating grin like the kind you can easily imagine drawn onto the cruel lips of medieval torturers. My fear, my pain, my horror, my sadness, my despair—those, I had decided, gave him pleasure far above the act of debasing me physically.

And so I refused to break down. Refused to give him the satisfaction of seeing me fear him. Refused to feel anything other than cold hatred for the man whose throat I would have slit with a grapefruit spoon if I'd known it wouldn't hurt my mother or interrupted my plans in life that had nothing to do with him, and which I would not let him undermine.

I stopped crying for at least ten years. Then, once the tears did start coming again—when he was a million light years and a trillion parsecs behind me—they wouldn't stop. To this day, I cry at kitten commercials.

And the pain? Well, it's just something that's there. I know it's there, and I know there's nothing I can do with it but accept its being there—and, in a way, thank it for being the fuel that reminds me always to be kind and never to forget that despair is a choice.

19

My Fellow Soldiers

THE NEXT MORNING BEFORE SURGERY, DR. Wiss and a small team of doctors and other medical personnel came in and asked if I'd yet seen the x-rays taken of my leg. I hadn't. He asked if I wanted to. I said yes. He asked if I had a strong stomach. I said I did—but even if I didn't, by now I needed to know what at least two doctors had already called the worst wound they'd seen outside of a war zone.

Dr. Wiss put the photos up on a light board and, before turning them toward me, actually let out a big sigh, knowing what he was about to do to my psyche.

Did I gasp? I'm not sure. But I for sure didn't puke. Now I knew what the worst injury short of a war wound looked like. Now I knew who the enemy was. And now, looking into their faces, I knew who my fellow soldiers were.

When Dr. Wiss said he was going to clean my leg up, it meant he was going to cut away the necrotic tissue. Until then, my leg was literally dying.

20

Perspective

I KNOW WHAT YOU'RE THINKING AND wondering. If I were you and reading this, I would too: *Why did she allow herself to be abused without telling anyone? Especially her mom, the person she should've told, no matter what that asshole told her he'd do.* I would, I'm sure, wonder that if I were you. Because, frankly, I wonder that about myself. But of course I'm looking back as an adult, which you likely are, with an adult's life perspective, which you likely have too.

As adults, we understand the past often feels clearer in memory than we experienced it in the moment. How often have you lie awake at night regretting not saying this or that to someone at the time? Few of us enjoy the gift of being entirely in the moment, with clarity of thought, all the time, never having to look back with regret at a misstep in action or a word improperly expressed in conversation.

Actually, I'm pretty sure none of us can say that about ourselves. None of us is entirely in the moment all of the time, with a clear mind and certainty of purpose. Most of us spend the majority of our lives either in the past or the future, regretting or ruminating something in the former, or imagining how the latter is going to be if only such-and such happens.

That's how it goes. So we can only do what we're capable of doing at any given moment, aware that we're likely to fall short, and forgiving ourselves our imperfections—which are entirely forgivable as long as we learn from our mistakes and do not knowingly make the same ones again.

As an adult.

Which I was not when that man who called himself my stepfather was abusing me. I was a young girl who trusted authority and believed in my parents to look after me. And when reality didn't coincide with the assumptions I made about the world, I had to rationalize reality.

Now that I'm an adult, a wife, a mother who would rather be eaten by fire ants for eternity than see harm come to either of my daughters, I understand why I used to be outraged beyond all imaginable comprehension by what this man did to me. But as a girl with no point of reference beyond my own experience and pain, I believed him when he said that he'd hurt my mother if I spoke up. Most people would. That's why so many of those young boys who were molested by priests said nothing year after year. Molesters use their victims' fear of harm coming to the one person whom they care about above all against them. Is this clever on their part or something they instinctively get about kids' nature? I don't know. I know only that I imagined he actually would harm my mother, and I cared about her well-being more than I cared about the abuse—that I recognized as abuse but knew I wouldn't die from—while I didn't know that about what I imagined he might do to her.

In a bout of weakness one day when I was ten or eleven, I told my dad what was happening with Chuck but also added, "He told me not to tell anybody, so don't tell anybody or he'll hurt Mom."

At the time, I really meant *Don't tell anybody.* I was

making him promise to keep a secret. It's not a secret I would've kept had I been the parent. But Dad did keep it.

I love my father. I love him deeply. And I honor him. But years later, when everyone knew, I asked him why he'd done nothing. I said "Why didn't you confront Chuck? Why didn't you tell Mom? Or the police?"

First he apologized, and did so abjectly. Then he said, "You told me not to."

For that matter, he may very well have wondered why I'd done nothing, this girl who was so mature she was cooking for her brothers and cleaning his house at age eight? What was my excuse beyond the crippling shame that seemed to come from every pore in my body every waking second of every day, and often in my dreams too?

Believe me, I think often about those days and wonder. The closest I can get to a reasonable rationale was a gut feeling that my mother, who is the salt of the earth, would have looked at me differently—that is, thought of me in a way I didn't want her to think of me. The only evidence I can offer, such as it is, was the time my brother somehow got his hands on a six-pack of beer and gave one to me. I'd never tasted alcohol before. Greenville was in a dry county, and it was a large county, so there wasn't as much alcohol as there otherwise might have been.

"Here," he said, "take one."

I took it and drank it, happy that finally, finally, finally my brother was being nice to me. But I should've known better. A couple of days later, I was in the bathroom getting dressed when Mom came in and said, "Cory told me about the beer."

The beer. Get it? One beer. Mine.

"My image of you is shattered," she said.

Shattered. Just like that. Her image of a girl who over-achieved in everything—all As in AP classes, worked to help pay for her own dance lessons, won state titles on the track team, had never given a moment's trouble—had been shattered.

"I thought you were my angel," she said, walking away.

That's all it took, one beer.

So maybe, possibly, I hadn't told her about what her husband was doing because I'd instinctively sensed her image of me would be shattered.

21

Small Victories

ALL RIGHT, SO THAT WAS ONE surgery down, X number to go.

It hurt. But nothing like it was soon to hurt.

A couple of hours into recovery some nurses came in to change the bandages. *Why did it take more than one?* I wondered. And they began.

The bandages had a kind of ointment between them and the skin, to make changing them easier. But removing them and re-adhering new ones required lifting my leg by the heel. And lifting it felt exactly like breaking it all over again. Which it was, in several places—wherever pins now held together the semblance of what had been, fifteen days prior, an intact leg. At the risk of sounding melodramatic, I feel confident in saying that drinking a sulfuric-acid smoothie with a lye chaser would have hurt less.

I had no power—and believe me, I tried—to stop the agonized scream from coming out of my body at full volume. It was autonomous, involuntary, like when the doctor taps under your knee with that hammer to check your reflexes.

I gripped the metal railings of the bed so hard I'm

surprised they didn't bend. Poor Johnny. He left the room—this being his wife's injury, not some nameless accident victim—but no matter where he was in the hospital, he could hear me. The only thing worse than being in pain yourself is hearing someone you love in pain.

When they finally were able to lift the bandage off, the nurses suggested I might not want to watch. No wonder. It looked like a live-action x-ray. What a hideous sight. We could see straight through my leg, or what little remained of my calf muscle, and note the striations. There were pins on top, near the knee, and two in the ankle, with steel rods tying them together. I could see exactly why it hurt when they moved it. I knew exactly what was happening every time, and why the bone was crumbling. Most distressing was I knew I had to face this agony every three hours around the clock.

The nurses were angels, and you can't get to heaven without being on their side. I wanted to be nice to them. I wanted to be glad to see them. And I most of all wanted them to be glad to see me. But I also knew pulling duty on my bandage changing every three hours was worse than cleaning latrines in the army—or, for that matter, changing diapers and emptying bedpans—if only because they'd have to endure the blood-curdling screams, knowing it had to be done and could never not be done, and certain that I dreaded seeing them come into the room. My anxiety became so bad I started keeping one eye on the clock in between sessions, which robbed me of the "good" moments I might otherwise have had with Johnny and my mother and the friends who came to visit.

The reality was I had no way out of this but through it. The only alternative was to let them take my leg, and that was no alternative at all.

For reasons I assume have entirely to do with my

survival instinct, I remembered an interview I'd heard on the radio when I first came to Los Angeles. It was with the actor who played the dad on the popular TV series *Family Ties*, Michael Gross, and I'm not sure if he was on the radio because he was promoting a book or being interviewed as a celebrity. I actually remember nothing else about the interview except the question the interviewer asked him about his lowest moment in life, which I thought was a strange thing to ask about. In retrospect, I realize it was something so out of the ordinary that it must have been a setup. I turned up the radio as I drove and listened hard. I'm glad I did. Mr. Gross told a fascinating story about getting fired from whatever acting job he had at the time on the same day he learned his wife had filed for divorce. Imagine that. What has stuck with me all these years hearing him say he recognized how, short of being hit by a meteor or getting cancer, his life had gotten about as bad as it could ever be. So he decided, that day, he would choose to do one thing, one simple thing, that was good for him; something that would improve his life. On that day, he said, he gave up smoking.

"But wasn't the stress of what you were going through exactly the kind of thing that made you want to smoke in the first place?" the interviewer asked, admitting he'd always been a nervous smoker himself. (I quote from memory.) "Wasn't it the kind of stress that smoking helps alleviate?"

"Yes, exactly, it is," Gross answered, "which was why I knew I needed to quit. Quitting, and exercising the self-discipline to quit, gave me some control over my horrible situation. Every day I didn't smoke was a small victory over the horror. And every day I didn't smoke I got that much better. In some weird way, I think it made quitting easier, because I knew how important it was to my mental health—much more than it was to my physical health. I haven't smoked since."

This story inspired me; in fact, I still remember what street I was driving down when I heard it. In my situation, with this awful leg, there was nothing I could do about my lower body. But I could still try to keep my upper body strong, and doing that would help me experience a sense of normalcy, which I needed at least as much as I needed to stay strong. Knowing I faced weeks, if not months, in the hospital—surgery after surgery after surgery, followed by a rehabilitation process that would be grueling, relentless, and painful—can take the joy out of waking every morning. I needed to do the things I loved doing, which was why I did them every day. And working out in any way, even if it was only a few curls, would be as close to normal as I would likely get for quite a while, given how many surgeries I faced in the coming months. So I called a friend from my gym and asked him to bring me some dumbbells that I could use while lying there. I used them religiously, devising new exercises aimed at working every possible muscle above my waist.

Then I asked the doctor if he would order a chin-up bar to be installed above my bed. He probably thought I was crazy, but I insisted, pointing out that I needed to keep up my upper-body strength.

The nurses favored this idea most and were the most grateful when the bar was finally installed. Can't say that I blame them. I was on an orthopedic floor filled almost entirely with elderly people who'd had some sort of joint replacement or had fallen and broken something. All of them, from what I heard, had to wear diapers, which meant someone had to change them. And someone had to wipe them. With my chin-up bar, however, I was able to lift myself off the bed and sit on the bedpan and do my business all on my own, leaving only the orderlies with the less-unpleasant task of emptying the waste. That made me a hero with the nurses even more than I already was for inviting them in to chitchat and make my room the place to sit a spell and shoot the breeze about life, love, and the rigors of the job.

I still laugh when I think about the time I'd lifted myself onto the pan to take a pee just as Dr. Wiss came in to talk. The whole time we talked, I pretended not to be sitting on a bedpan, and he pretended not to notice.

22
Hidden Blessings

UNTIL DIABETES AND HEART ISSUES CAUGHT up to him, my grandfather, Jim Crofford, was as strong as my grandmother, Big Granny—and as stubborn as I am, which is why, at eighty-five, his diabetes and heart issues caught up with him. He'd spent decades as a supervisor with the Texas Department of Transportation, so when I was growing up, every time I drove or walked or rode anywhere, I assumed I was on his territory.

Growing up, I thought of my grandfather as the best man I knew. So why didn't I confide in him about what Mom's husband was doing to me? The answer is, frankly, that I worried more about what my grandfather thought of me than what anyone else in my life thought. I was so ashamed of what was happening, I couldn't bear the possibility that my grandfather might start thinking less of me. No, I didn't worry he'd blame me for what was happening. I worried his image of me would somehow be tainted; that he'd look at me differently.

Such was the insidiousness of Chuck's abuse. It was so shameful to me, I worried that his shame might rub off on me, at least as far as my grandfather was concerned. In my mind, it was possible it could have shattered what he thought of me. He went to his grave, bless his soul, not knowing about it, and when he died, I was the only one of my siblings who received something from his will. I got his boots, which he knew I would know were among the most valuable and meaningful of all his possessions.

As weird as it may be to say this, I believe the pain and isolation I felt back then were an ironic blessing of sorts. When you know from an early age that you're on your own and can rely only and entirely on yourself, it's as liberating as it is sad. But if you can take the sadness and self-pity out of it, then what you're left with is a liberating sense of freedom—and, when trauma strikes, you don't waste any time looking for someone to bail you out.

23
Attitude of Gratitude

GROWING UP, I DIDN'T KNOW THERE was any other way to be in life than completely self-sufficient. Johnny still talks about how when we first started dating my air conditioner's compressor went on the fritz. He walked in and there I was with my tools, trying to fix it. In his shock he asked, "What are you doing?"

"What do you mean?" I answered. "I'm fixing it."

"You have a toolbox? You know how to fix stuff?"

He was floored. (And, he loved it.)

"Sure I have a toolbox. Of course I know how to fix things."

"Well," he said, "from now on, you can get rid of your toolbox and use *my* toolbox."

He was of course referring to a real toolbox, one filled with wrenches and screwdrivers and ratchet sets. But it was also a vivid and fitting metaphor. For the first time in my life, I was with someone who could not only take care of himself but who wanted to take care of me too, and was eminently capable of doing so. Nonetheless, it took me a long time to let him. There was a lot to overcome, and the process of letting go would be incremental.

"I am *not* getting rid of my toolbox," I said, though I

admit to feeling a tug of vulnerability—and not disliking it.

All things considered, I'd rather by far have been taught self-reliance first, before learning somehow to be vulnerable and accept help, than to have been taught to always expect help and then be forced by unplanned circumstances to learn self-reliance.

It was my base of self-reliance that kept me going when I lie in the dark (or as dark as hospital rooms get—so, not very dark) in the wee hours, watching infomercials about achieving that perfect Brazilian butt, and contemplating what the future held for me, which was now going to be substantially different than how I'd anticipated my future to look until one second before the accident.

Now, not only was I never going to have that perfect Brazilian butt, but I may lose my leg. That, obviously, was still an authentic possibility. Dr. Wiss had made clear he could make no assurances, as there was no guarantee I'd be able to live with what would be ongoing pain for the type that made ordinary arthritis seem like bruised feelings.

There was no way around the fact that my days of modeling and being in fitness videos were over, even if I kept my leg and even if I could live with the pain, because this leg was never again going to be shapely and cosmetically attractive—even if the greatest plastic surgeon on earth took over after Dr. Wiss did his job.

Depression began to kick in, the kind that kicks your butt, drags you naked over cobblestones, and throws you to the wolves while you're still alive. It was awful. It was debilitating. It was as terrifying as a glimpse into the abyss. But because of my upbringing, I didn't bother with the self-pity, which is where most people who are depressed after accident or misfortune get bogged down, sometimes forever. *Why me? Woe is me.* Since I don't have that learned behavior, my instinct was to *do something* about the depression. That's my coping mechanism.

I opened my journal and immediately began a gratitude list—that is, all the things for which I was grateful. So instead of staring into darkness, I focused on what was light in my life. Ruby. Savanna. Johnny. My family. My friends. My home. Swimming. Nature. Blue skies. Clouds. Birds singing. Music. America. The career I'd worked so hard for. Everything I'd overcome and achieved. My health, aside from this damn leg. Yet even that, too, made the list, because I still had my leg, for which I was grateful. If it hadn't been for the right doctor being on-call at the right time, I'd now be staring down at a stump. I was grateful for Dr. Jabour.

The list got longer and longer, and the longer it got, the less depressed I got. The self-administered medicine was working, as intended. Psychological depression, as opposed to biochemical depression, doesn't occur in a vacuum. It occurs in negativity, when "what I don't have" seems greater than "what I want to have." All things considered, I had far more to be grateful about than I had to moan about. I knew if any one of the items on that list (only part of which I've included here) had been taken away from me, I'd feel the loss far more deeply than any agony I now found myself in. One thing I know for sure about life is that the true state of our condition is never known to us until illustrated by its contrary. We human beings rarely know how to value what we have until we lose it. And I was determined to beat those odds by listing and acknowledging all my blessings. Gratitude turns denial into acceptance, makes sense of our past, brings peace for today, and creates hope for tomorrow.

I even began including on my list every visit from a nurse, regardless of whether she made me scream in pain. In fact, I wanted to make sure the nurses knew they were welcome in my room, that I appreciated what they were doing for me, and that I never wanted them to not come in. So somehow I managed to turn my room into party central. Mine was the only room that had a small refrigerator in it, and my wonderful friends were always bringing me organic foods and juices and also nonorganic cakes and cookies—far more than I could ever eat. The nurses would come in, have something to eat or drink, and many would pour their hearts out to me. Boyfriend problems, girlfriend problems, husband problems, children problems, life-in-general problems. We'd talk and talk, and soon I found myself with a reputation for handing out common-sense advice of exactly the kind of thing my grandmothers had given me. I think I was channeling them when I did it because some of the nurses would come to me later and thank me for what turned out to be good guidance: Never give up hope.

Then, seeing how assiduously I was working out with the weights and chin-up bar—and thankful to me for not having to change a diaper—they began coming in to see if I'd devise exercise routines for them. They'd do it at all hours of the night, knowing that the pain was keeping me up anyway and, I'm sure, believing I'd be grateful for the distraction. I was. I'd write out full plans for them to follow.

Unsolicited, I then began writing down exercise plans for my clients, exercise plans for my friends and family, and did anything I could think of to be of service to others instead of lying there thinking about myself and my situation. There were plenty of medical people I trusted to worry about me, and plenty of loved ones doing the same. I didn't need to worry about myself. What I needed was to take the focus off of me and put it on others. Even though I couldn't get up and get out of this bed—yet!—I could still be useful in the world. That was my attitude.

24

Need to Be the Best

I'M AS COMPETITIVE AS ANYONE YOU'VE ever met, and have never not been. It's my nature. Even as a little kid, I always wanted to run faster, jump higher, catch more bugs, and get the most Halloween candy. In truth, I wasn't even into eating the Halloween candy as much as I was into getting more than anyone else I went trick-or-treating with. I did, though, have a bug collection that I wanted to be the most impressive of anyone's—impressive enough that kids and adults who both did and didn't have bug collections would still be impressed by. I found a big cigar box in which I pinned them and wrote what kind of bug it was underneath in tiny letters. At the time, I thought I'd be able to combine dancing with science, working as either an entomologist or an archeologist, both of those professions spent largely outside, which appealed to me but which was completely ironic because dancing is done indoors unless you have a gig on an outdoor stage.

That competitiveness was what made me such a good runner. At school meets, I ran the half mile, the mile, the two-mile, and sometimes the break between those races was only a few minutes. I'd still be breathing hard from the previous race, and I used to wonder how I'd even complete the next race, let alone win. It made me so nervous, I often threw up right before. But when the gun went off, something would happen inside me, and all that tiredness disappeared behind my need to be the best. After winning a state district record in the mile, my coach began pulling me out of academic classes, insisting the school was counting on me to win state. "You're our only hope," she'd say. Later, she encouraged me to start thinking about, and training for, the Olympics. That was her dream, though, not mine.

When it became clear I had to choose between running and dance—because I couldn't devote the time necessary to bring home gold to the school, let alone make the Olympics, and also dance the way I wanted to—I broke my coach's heart, or so she said, and chose dance.

25

Love and Pain

I HAD KEPT A JOURNAL MOST of my life until the mid-1990s, then picked it up again around the time Johnny and I met, writing in a flurry for a while and stopping for reasons I can't remember. But now, being confined to a hospital bed seemed like an auspicious time to again start recording my thoughts and feelings.

I asked Johnny to bring my journal from home, asking him not to peek inside, though I knew he probably would have anyway (and now for sure would because I'd asked him not to). Over the next few months, there was going to be plenty of time for writing, and while it may then have seemed like I'd never forget a single second, I was determined to put this place and this experience so far in my rearview memory that I knew there'd come a day when it would rekindle memories otherwise lost in the ether. In fact, I opened to the first page and immediately got caught up in what I'd written years before, never at the time believing I'd forget it:

May 20, 2006.
How things change. For the first time in years, I feel safe. I feel peace. I think I have found my dream man.

Johnny. Superhero Johnny. Is this real? Is he really the one? It feels so right. I pray it's right. I think I love him, and I know I want him to love me. I really want a healthy relationship. And I'm ready for it. So, what I must find out is, can he love me for me?

It went on like that for another couple of pages, with me weighing the pros and cons, and trying to guess, then second-guess, his intent. Despite the pain in my leg I got immersed in the love story, as if I didn't know how it ended.

The next entry wasn't until two weeks later.

June 2, 2006.
Well, it has been the most blissful, amazing last month. My life is wonderful. I am in love. And the love is strong, so strong. I had a fantastic time with Johnny—and more lovin' than I have ever had in my life. I sit in my fancy hotel room in Long Beach overlooking the ocean. This has been the first alone time I have had in probably a month. I think of how lucky I am; how fortunate I've been; how grateful I am for everything. I never thought I would get married again, but I would love to call Johnny my husband. I am so proud of him. He is truly amazing. I want this to last forever.

I don't know why, but not till August 2 did I write again.
My life is good. For the first time since Savanna was born, I am thinking of having a baby. I love Johnny. I want to have his baby. I want him to be the father of my baby.

I meant no disrespect to Savanna's father, my ex-husband. But with him, I'd had neither the maturity nor the depth of emotion for him to have been excited this way about starting a family. I loved Savanna with all my heart, but her father and I, as events subsequently proved, were a poor match.

Much happened between that August 2 when I declared, on paper, my love for Johnny and the following entry, dated "January 2009"—not sure which day.

It's been a while. A marriage and a baby later. Things are so wonderful. Ruby Lee Rose is soooooo beautiful.

My eyes filled with tears, less from pain in my leg than from emotion. Oh, Ruby.

Seeing that, I realized I absolutely had to begin recording this journey I was now being forced to take, if only as documentation to share later with my little girl. So, I began with the last date I could remember—May 28—and wrote, *The day of the accident.* That's all. No other comment. No other comment necessary; the rest of the page was blank.

Atop the following page I wrote, *May 29. Coma.*

Then, *May 30. ICU.*

At last came a page with no date but the notation on the top line, *Transferred to Cedars-Sinai.*

The next few pages in the journal are blank except for the days of the week written atop each. I imagine I either had nothing to say or was in too much pain to express it properly.

Monday June 7 surgery. THIRD surgery day.

Tuesday June 8.
PAIN
PAIN
PAIN

And then—finally:

Wednesday June 9. This is the best day I have had. I finally slept about five hours last night. I woke up and showed the doctor that I could do a pull up, and he took the catheter out of me! Yay!!! I have been sitting in a chair for over an hour, and just went to the bathroom for the first time in almost two weeks without a catheter. I cannot express how utterly amazing that felt. I almost felt like a human being again. It's the small things that we take for granted. I won't ever do that again—I hope. I have already learned I need to slow down and really appreciate what I have. And oh my God, Johnny has been so unbelievably wonderful.

The next day, June 10, was even better. But to understand why, you need some background. The nurses had told me that children under a certain age—and Ruby, at two, was well below that age—weren't allowed in the ICU rooms. So, the only way I was going to be able to see her was if I could sit up in a wheelchair and be rolled out to the waiting room. I said fine, sure, I'll do it, because I'd do anything humanly possible to see my little girl. We'd never been apart, and here it was two weeks since my accident.

When I say I tried, believe me, I tried. And as anyone who knows me well knows I can try as hard as I think Navy SEALs try. The nurse would come in and I'd push myself as the screams from godawful pain escaped involuntarily. Johnny had to leave the room and went down to the cafeteria. The nurse looked at the monitor with my vital signs and saw my heart rate tripling, my blood pressure doubling, and said, "Let's do this again another day."

I said, "No, I want to do this," and I tried, but I still couldn't. Same result.

As it happened, down in the cafeteria where he'd gone to escape my agony, Johnny ran into Dr. Wiss eating soup. Johnny explained why he was down there, and Dr. Wiss picked up two of those small cellophane-wrapped packs of Saltine crackers. The first one he broke into halves, and said, "This is an ordinary break." Then he picked up the second pack, crumbled it in his hand, and said, "This is your wife's leg." To move it was to re-break it.

Which was why I couldn't manage to sit up no matter how many times I tried. Which was why the nurses decided to band together and break the rules in a way that might prevent any of them from getting in trouble.

They told Johnny when to bring Ruby and promised they'd all guard the door, making sure no hospital administrator or charge nurse came by to toss her out. It had been two weeks to the day since my little girl and I had seen each other.

Anticipating this moment, I'd of course imagined her running and jumping into my arms. But that's not what happened. Poor Ruby. Even though I'd put on makeup for the first time since the accident, trying to look as normal as possible, there was no getting past the huge bandage on my legs and the IV in my arm. She looked so scared. "Mama," she said, pointing at my leg, "boo boo," she said.

"Yeah," I said, "big boo boo."

She'd always been a mama's girl, and now you could see she was afraid to climb in my bed with me. I thought she was going to cry, and my first instinct was to try to distract her, the way you do with kids when they fall and bleed a little. So, I immediately looked to see what was at hand on my bedside table. There were some candies friends had brought me, and some nail polish from another friend. Ruby loved when I painted her nails, and like all kids, she loved candy. So those are what I used to lure her into bed with me.

She also liked all the buttons—one to call the nurse, one to call the doctor, one to dispense the dilaudid that kept my pain at a semi-endurable level. That last one was the one she kept pushing, and I didn't care how many times she did it as long as she was in the bed with me. Believe me, I was loopy by the time she left, but I needed to see her. It reminded me, not that I needed reminding, why I absolutely had to get well and not give in to either the pain or the despair.

We snuck Ruby in!!! I wrote in my diary. She was scared at first to see me and said she wanted Daddy. But after five minutes, she ended up staying in bed with me for two hours. She didn't want to leave, and I didn't want her to. I just wanted to keep holding her, and keep that moment going forever. When she gave me goodbye kisses, my heart melted. My mom had to trick her into leaving by telling her they had to look for kittens outside. I cried.

I later wrote some more.

June 11, 2010.
Day of fourth surgery. I'm so thirsty and nervous. I wasn't nervous in my second surgery because I thought I would wake up with no pins. Wrong! I pray I wake up this time without them. They are going in to replace my fibula and fix my tibia.

At six that night, in a different-colored ink, I wrote,

OMG! The pain is horrible. Came out of surgery at 11:15 but had to stay in recovery until 2 PM. They couldn't seem to get my pain under control. Finally, at 5 PM, the pain started getting better. The kitchen has still not brought me any food. Thank God my mom went downstairs and got me a sandwich. We had asked so many times. I'm so drowsy, I can barely write...

And the next day,

June 12.
Didn't sleep one wink last night. Still in pain and hoping it will ease up. Even if it eases a little, I'll be so grateful. Mom left this morning, and I'm sad about that. Savanna slept with me last night and really helped. She had to hand me my bed pan probably ten times. I'm disappointed she isn't spending the night tonight. But she's tired, very tired. She needs to sleep. I so appreciate what she did.

Johnny is fantastic. If not for him, I would right now be crying over the leg I don't have and learning to live with only one.

Wait, maybe the pain is starting to let up.
No, never mind.

The following day I wrote a much longer entry.

June 13, 2010.
Well, I got about six hours of sleep. Yay. I feel like a new person. Woke up at six and braided my hair and actually put a little makeup on. It's amazing how a little makeup and a little sleep can make you feel so much better, like a human being again. I'd always heard that when you don't feel normal, just do something normal and you'll feel more normal.

Turns out, it works. Of course, it's a lot easier being normal when you (a) can sleep, and (b) aren't in pain. Johnny slept over last night. I could not possibly ask for a better husband. He went to get us some coffee, which was okay because I had already had blood and vital signs taken, and pushed my pain button a whole bunch of times. I'm trying to push it as little as possible, but when I don't the pain is indescribable.

"I already cannot count or remember how many times I have been poked since I got to the hospital. My right arm and hand are black and blue.

It's still amazing to me how one single solitary second can change your life. I'm looking at the clock, shocked at how almost routine all this surgery stuff has become. They come in and take blood, which sucks since my picc line [short for a percutaneous indwelling catheter, a kind of semi-permanent catheter that's intended to make it easy to inject everything from medication to chemotherapy drugs—if that's what's needed] doesn't work well for that. They give me meds—one pill for nerve pain, two pills for all-over pain, two Tylenol, and another pill to make me poop, which I may never do again because of all the opiates in my system.

The clock says 11:45. Only fifteen more minutes for me to have something to eat or drink, and here I am writing instead of eating or drinking. At 12, I can't have any more food or drink, not even water. I'm nervous about tomorrow's surgery—scared I'm going to wake up in so much pain again. I feel like I've been through hell and am making my way back. Last time I had surgery, it took them three hours to get my pain under control. God, please please please help me make it through tomorrow without that happening again, or if it does happen again, please give me the strength and the will to endure it. They are replacing—or actually putting in—a metal plate to fix my tibia near my ankle.

"I am so lucky, I know I am, to still have my leg. I praise God. I am so lucky, I know I am, even to be alive. I praise God for that too. But tonight I began to think about what beautiful legs I've always had, legs for which I've always been known professionally, and the compliments I've always gotten when I wear shorts and dresses and skirts—the compliments I'll never get again unless it's someone telling me how much they admire me for not caring about letting such a messed-up leg show. So I guess I now have to change my wardrobe to things that will cover my leg.

"Well, that's getting way, way ahead of myself. First let me make sure I'm keeping the leg. Then let me walk. Then get me out of this hospital. Then I'll worry about what my leg looks like and what I wear.

And now that I've gotten that off my chest, I hope I sleep. It's too late to eat and drink.

Early the following morning, before surgery, I wrote again.

June 14, 2010.
I slept fine except for the nurses waking me every hour on the hour. Then they woke me at five for surgery, which isn't till 7:15. The first thing they did was take blood. And yes, of course, my picc line doesn't work, so they have to draw blood. I look like a junkie with

so many bruises on both arms. (Do junkies have bruises?)

Oh, God, I'm praying so hard I don't hurt as bad this time when I come out of surgery. I feel like a torture victim who knows that at any minute they may come for him again. Yes, I know that the intentional infliction of pain for torture and the accidental infliction of pain in order to hurt you are completely different, but I can't imagine that being put on the rack hurts any more than what's happened to me. So God, please, have mercy. I'm so scared. This is the first time I've been by myself. And I pray I will be strong. I know I'm in good hands. And I trust the doctors and nurses.

Good thing I'm going to be asleep for a while because I'm already so hungry and thirsty I could chug a whole liter of water and scarf down a whole meal, but I won't be able to eat or drink anything for at least another ten hours. This just adds to the torture.

I'll try to write later, if I'm not in too much pain.

Later that night:

PAIN PAIN PAIN. Five-hour surgery. They put a metal plate on my tibia by the ankle. Didn't get out of recovery until 3 PM.

What an experience. What an experience. What an experience. And I think I've been pretty strong throughout this whole ordeal. In my moments of weakness or feeling depressed, I just start writing in this journal about everything I'm thankful for.

I have so many people in my life to be grateful for, and have been blessed in so many ways. I see now that all those years of dancing and running and working through pain and discomfort have prepared me for what I'm going through. When I danced, my feet always hurt. My feet were like a boxer's hands, so callused that I could be on point shoes with no padding. All those beatings I took from my brother, they toughened me up and taught me to keep going. Running track in a hundred degrees with 90 percent humidity, you didn't get to make excuses. I ran and kept running no matter what, not even stopping to puke. I would just do it as I ran. And then there was Chuck, learning to take what he did, put it into a tiny compartment in my mind, close the door, and lock it. My whole childhood was about sucking up pain, physical, emotional, psychological. It was about always having to think that what I did today would pay off tomorrow. Now, all those different kinds of pain are there for me to deal with again—times a thousand. I can do it. And I can do it because I have done it. And I can do it, I know I can do it, because there's no alternative to doing it. Same as ever.

But there's also something else I'm grateful for: my sense of humor. My client Nicole called me today and was super upset because she just found out that she was pregnant. She was crying about it, wondering how she was going to deal with another new baby now. I waited till she was done, then told her I was in the hospital because of a motorcycle accident, almost lost my leg, but was about to have yet another surgery on it and would probably be in the hospital for several more weeks, if not months, and at best would never really be able to walk completely normally again— and according to the doctors would never not be in pain.

She said, "I'm not ready for this," and started crying again. Was she kidding? I said she should celebrate this wonderful thing, bringing a life into the world. But she kept crying. I don't think she heard a word I said about my own issue, or if she did being pregnant seemed like a lot worse news to her. By the end of the conversation I was trying to make her feel better by promising to come over and babysit for her. If I can walk by then.

26

Stubbornly Game

SO MUCH ABOUT THE HOSPITAL EXPERIENCE, whether it lasts days, weeks, or months, is about dealing with indignities and humiliation. A part of you has to readjust your expectations of propriety. You have no choice. But in my case, that was particularly hard because since childhood, for good reasons, I never quite relax in the bathroom—if you know what I mean—when anyone is within two zip codes. Really, even if I only have to pee when people are in my living room, I'll go upstairs rather than use my powder room.

As strange as it sounds, in some ways being that vulnerable was one of the best things to happen to me. It forced me to ask for help when needed, taught me how to receive help when it's given, and how to admit out loud when I needed help. These were what I'd had problems with since I learned from childhood to put a lid on things without complaint or acknowledgment.

For example, one Saturday night when I was sixteen, I was involved in a pretty bad car accident. The day before was the last day of school before summer, so everyone was in a rowdy mood. I was riding shotgun in my best friend's car on a highway outside of town. She turned left in front of an oncoming truck going sixty miles an hour. *Wham!* My head went through the windshield, and when I tried to get out of what remained of her car, I felt something cold on my feet. It was my blood. I couldn't stand up, and was obviously in shock when the paramedics came because I told them I was fine. "No, you're not," they said, and helped me out of the car into the ambulance. Every place they touched me hurt—wrist, leg, head, back.

X-rays were taken in the emergency room when we arrived. My leg pain was excruciating. Afterward, I called Mom to pick me up. A wheelchair aide took me to her car. Once we got home, Chuck carried me into the house because I still couldn't walk. That, more than anything, should explain how bad my leg was, my agreeing to let him carry me. But I refused to let him take me as far as my bedroom down the hall. I told him to set me on the couch in the living room. That's where I spent the night, not sleeping because of the leg pain, and throwing up from what was obviously an undiagnosed concussion.

The next morning Mom told me to hurry and put on my Sunday best for church. I said, "Mom, I can't even walk."

She didn't say, "Oh, my God, we better get you checked." Or, "Let me call the hospital and see if they found anything." Instead, she insisted I get dressed and go with her. But I told her no, pointing to my leg, which I obviously wouldn't even be able to put my pantyhose over.

"Okay," she said. "I guess you can miss church this one time."

I asked her to pick up some crutches for me on the way home. She did.

Unfortunately, the timing was particularly bad for me, not because I couldn't enjoy the summer, but because on Saturday I had a dance solo in the recital at which I was being presented as a teacher for the dance academy. I had trained for two years to make this happen. Not only did I not want to let myself down, but I didn't want to let down my teacher, Jackie Nutting, who also hailed from the University of Suck It Up; in fact, she'd gotten her PhD. I'd decided I wanted to model myself around Jackie—how she thought, how she lived, how she worked, how she was. I adored her. I remember when I'd felt so proud of myself for being able to do four pirouettes on the left side, and she said, "You can always do more." And when I took her teacher training program to qualify as a teacher and earn money from it, she began by telling everyone in the class, "I don't care what you have going on in your life. I don't care if your dog or your best friend just died, you come to class ready to teach. The second you put the needle on the record and turn to your students, you wear a smile on your face and do your job."

So, when, at rehearsal Monday morning, she saw me on crutches and asked if I was going to be ready to go on Saturday, I said yes, absolutely, definitely. And I meant it. Even if I couldn't rehearse that day, and even when it turned out my leg still hurt too much the next day, I was not going to fail myself or her. With or without rehearsal, I was going to nail this performance at the municipal auditorium.

An hour before curtain, I put down the crutches and tried for the first time since the accident to put weight on it, preparing to dance on it. The pain was as if someone had hit me with a flamethrower. How was I going to be able to do a Can-Can, which takes a lot of bouncing, one leg to the other, when I couldn't even stand? I didn't know, but the show had to go on, and I figured that when the curtain rose, so would the pain-deadening adrenaline.

"Are you sure you can go?" Jackie asked.

"Yes, absolutely," I answered.

In the past when I'd complained about my feet bleeding from dancing in point shoes, she'd tell me to suck it up and keep dancing, so that's what I intended to do. I began strapping on my high-heeled pump until my grandmother came running backstage and told me to stop.

It seems she'd gotten a call from my mother, who'd been tracked down at work by the hospital (this being a small town, everyone was always only one or two degrees of separation from someone who knew how to get to someone). Finally, a doctor at the hospital had read my X-rays and determined that I'd broken my fibula, the small bone, in my left leg. Back then, the local hospital didn't necessarily have every kind of specialty present every minute.

The radiologist or orthopedic surgeon, or whoever picked up the pictures off that desk that morning, must've been surprised to see that someone in town had been walking around for more than three days on a leg that should've already been in a cast. He'd then called around until finding my mother at work, who called my grandmother because she worked nearer to the auditorium, and asked her to come tell me to get off that leg. If my grandmother hadn't shown up exactly when she did, I'd have gone out there, gutted it out, and quite possibly really screwed myself up by turning this clean break halfway up the fibula into a compound fracture, with the top pushing through my skin.

One of the problems with having such a high pain threshold, and being so stubbornly game, is that you can do real damage to yourself by not listening to your body's signals. Jack Youngblood, a Hall of Fame defensive end for the Los Angeles Rams, played the 1980 Super Bowl on a broken fibula—enduring unimaginable pain—because he'd already seen the doctor who'd put my leg in a temporary brace and told him not to worry about doing any more damage to it;

the damage had already been done. "As long as you can stand the pain, and I don't see how you can," the doc said, "feel free to play."

When I got to the hospital with my leg I knew was broken, the new doctor began prepping me for a cast. I asked how long it would have to be there. Six weeks, he said.

I said, "What if I promise not to walk on my leg all that time? Can I get away without the cast?"

For a dollar, the local country club let anyone come in and use the pool. My friends and I would spend half the summer swimming, and if I had a cast on I wouldn't be able to go in. Believe me, in Texas in the summer, you want to be able to get relief from the heat. I also didn't mention that in a few weeks I had a dance competition coming up, and after missing the performance earlier that day, I wasn't about to miss the competition.

"All right," he said. "But you make sure to stay off it for six weeks. No weight bearing. And I want to see you back here then."

"Absolutely," I said.

In about three weeks I threw the crutches away, and competed in the competition. And in about three months the pain stopped too. I never went back.

27

Tomorrow is Another Day

June 16, 2010.

I'M SO THIRSTY!

Having another surgery. Surprise! They are going in to clean up everything and take out one wound vacuum.

THIS IS MY 6TH SURGERY!!!!!!

Sixth. Six surgeries. Six. I can't believe it myself.

But my prayers, I think, are being answered. I am feeling a bit better. This is the first surgery that resulted in a pain level not above a 3-5. Finally! Maybe I'll even be able to sleep tonight.

Well, here's something to laugh about. I mean, it could've been horrible, but now it's something to laugh about. My friend Michelle had brought me some photos of Ruby and Savanna and a scented candle—kind of like a little shrine. It was so wonderful. My eyes filled when I saw it. So we lit the candle, and a while later one of the male nurses came in and said, "Wow, it smells really good in here." I said, "Thank you." He asked what it's from. I pointed to the candle. He said, "Oh, my God. Are you crazy? There's oxygen in here. You could've blown up the hospital." He took the candle out of here before blowing it out, then brought it back without the wick. I guess he didn't trust me. So now I just stick my nose in and sniff. It still smells good.

Savanna spent the night. She brought Starbucks coffee this morning, and I talked to Ruby on the phone. She told Johnny that Mommy's feeling better. Oh, my heart.

———

June 18, 2010.

Went in for surgery at 8:30 and got out by two. Oh my God, it hurts so much. They went in to clear everything out in preparation for Monday's surgery. I don't remember a day in my life when I cried more than today. Because there hasn't been one. And there was also never a day when I cried from being in actual physical pain. I didn't even know that crying from pain helps the pain. Well, it doesn't. But I couldn't stop myself.

I felt so bad lying here crying while Johnny was here, sleeping over, trying to get some sleep. I wanted to be with him, but all I could do was cry. He couldn't sleep with me crying. Of course he couldn't. He didn't know what to do. He just wanted to take my pain away from me. I could see it was making him crazy, not being able to help. Johnny is not the type of man who can just shrug his shoulders when his wife is in torment. He has to Do Something. But there was nothing to do. I finally sent him home. He didn't want to go. I begged him. He needs to sleep. So do I. But after three weeks, I'm used to the sleepless nights and the nurses coming in every hour and waking me up, even if I do happen to fall asleep. He's not. And why should everyone be miserable just because I have to be? Their being in misery, too, doesn't make me feel any better. It actually makes me feel worse, knowing that my pain is inflicting pain on someone else, especially someone I love. If I were the only person in the world in pain, I wouldn't want anyone else to be pain, not even a stranger. What a weird thing that is to think. I know they say that misery likes company. But why? How does that help? Especially if my pain is the cause of their pain. No, the only way for me to feel better is for me to feel better. And I'm determined to do that.

———————

June 19, 2010.

They brought me in a walker today. OMG! OMG! OMG! On the one hand (or leg), it was amazing to stand up for the first time in almost a month, even if it was on just one leg. On the other hand, the pain was amazing. All the blood, from gravity, rushed to the leg the way it does whenever you stand. But after all this time, and all that has happened, it felt like a freight train under my skin. I wanted so bad to walk, just walk—walk like I have since I was ten months old, even when I broke my leg as a teenager—from here to there. But all I could do, because of the pain, was stand there. Or try to. Again, it made me cry, and feel like a failure.

"I'm so tired. So tired I can hardly write. Too tired to think. Too tired to do anything. But as Scarlett O'Hara said, "Tomorrow is another day."

———————

June 20, 2010.

YAY! It's Father's Day—and I was able to walk with the walker all the way around my bed to the door and back. Yes, it was on one leg. And I hopped. But it was incredible, truly incredible. The look on Johnny's face, this being Father's Day, said that watching me "walk" was the best possible present I could have given him.

My physical therapist had to tell me to slow down because he couldn't keep up. The pain was excruciating. But I didn't care. I just wanted to keep going. I was determined, and as long as I knew I wasn't doing any damage to the leg, that it was only pain, I knew I needed to complete the journey to my destination. These were my first steps of a thousand-mile journey, even if the foot wasn't touching the ground, and if I didn't take those steps now, when would I? And if I never took them, I'd never get anywhere.

Another wonderful thing happened today too. After I took those steps, I was able to get into a wheelchair. Actually, I demanded that they let me try to get into a wheelchair, which they didn't want to do, but I insisted, so finally the doctors and nurses agreed to let me take a shot at it. It's amazing what cabin fever will do for your level of motivation. I needed to be out of this room beyond being wheeled out on a gurney for surgery, then back in after recovery. Yes, it hurt. It hurts whenever the leg is down. But in the wheelchair I was able to have my leg propped up and out straight in front of me and go to the plaza level and then outside. The second the nurse dropped me off downstairs, and I could feel the sun on my face and the wind through my hair, I began crying tears of happiness. I was so grateful. I felt free, which is funny considering I can't walk and may not be able to walk for a long, long time. But I was, I was free. I immediately pushed myself all over the place, smiling at everybody. I even found myself racing this little old man who was barely hobbling along in his robe. Being in this wheelchair was like an E-ticket ride at Disneyland.

Again, it is so obvious to me that we do not know what we have at any given moment of our lives until it's snatched away, and I just treasured those moments today—moments that wouldn't even have been moments in ordinary life. They'd have been time spent in transit on the way to doing something else. Please, Amberly, remember this. Remember these feelings and realizations and hold on to them always.

I'll try. But I know it will be hard. I know I'll forget. I

know I'll be distracted. I know people always try to remember these things when they have a life-changing event and want to never forget what they felt and thought. And that's why I'm writing them down.

I also want to remember that I beat that little old man who didn't know he was racing me.

———————

June 21, 2010.

Today is the day of my big surgery! What I just found out this morning is that they have to take muscle from either my latissimus dorsi or my calf. Hopefully, it'll be my calf, not my back, but after three weeks of inactivity, I'm worried that there's not enough muscle in my calf anymore. If there's not enough there, then they might have to take from my abs in order to fill in the two holes in my leg that are too big to fill in without a skin graft. That would add insult to injury. I know my leg is going to look messed-up forever, so I really don't want both my front and back to be too. But I guess that's out of my hands. Apparently you can see right into my leg when you look into the holes. I thought about asking for a mirror to see what they're talking about, but what would be the point? Our skin is supposed to protect us, and when it's not there, bad things happen. The risk of infection is incredibly high, and if it gets into my bones, that would be the end.

I will have to be in ICU tonight, so they can keep a close eye on me to make sure the muscle takes. I just shaved my legs and realized that this is the last day I'll ever again look at my right thigh without seeing huge scars, and maybe even gouges. Of course, below the knee already looks like a Picasso, so what's the difference? Be positive, Amberly, be positive.

Just two days ago I was feeling so happy and full of light.

Oh, well. Life is a seesaw. If you go up, you have to come down. And if you're never down, you can't go up. Yes, you can get off the seesaw. When you die.

Oh, Lord help me, please. I am scared of what's going to happen.

———

June 22, 2010.

This was the worst day yet. By far. And that is really saying something. I haven't felt pain like this in my life, not even last week. Oh, my God, it's horrible. How much can I take? I feel like I'm being tested. And failing. I am in too much pain even to write. I can't move my body at all because it hurts so much. Why aren't the pain meds working? Has my body gotten so used to them they don't work anymore?

I can't even write, which my body wants me to do, because I'm not allowed to move my legs because of the skin grafts. They could rub off or something. How much longer can this go on? How much longer can I go like this?

Savanna will spend the night, but no other visitors. Too much pain. Too much pain. Too much pain.

———

June 23, 2010.

I slept horribly, in and out all night, never getting to that good restful sleep, only a kind of narcotic haze from all the medication. But even that was broken up by the nurses coming in and out all night.

Mostly what disturbed me was thinking about the accident itself. Every time I closed my eyes, I would see the moment of impact happen all over again, so I became scared to close my eyes. I wrote the word *angry* in my journal several times because, I believe for the first time since that day, I allowed myself to feel seriously angry at the man who hit me. But it was more than that. I was angry that I was stuck in this hospital bed. I was angry that I was stuck in this body that was broken. I was angry that I had to practice patience.

Boy, was I angry. Incensed. Irate. Livid. Fuming. Furious. But I was also hurt that I hadn't heard from him, hadn't received an apology, not even a note of regret. Nothing. No communication. Which had the effect of leaving me with the vivid, indelible memory of his face as he stood there on the street with his arms crossed, looking not horrified but inconvenienced.

A bit of human kindness would have been the least he could have shown, and would have gone a long way toward making me feel better about the consequences of his actions that I'd be living with forever. My God, he didn't have to show up at the hospital, hat in hand, and fall on his knees, begging for forgiveness and mercy. All he had to do was send a small note saying nothing more than he hoped I would be back on my feet soon or that I should feel better. A sentiment like that wouldn't have suggested guilt, and couldn't be inferred as such. Maybe it would have given a measure of peace to both of us.

But as I stared down at the bandages covering what the plastic surgeon had done for the graft, knowing that I'd been disfigured on my thigh too, to protect the lower leg that was no longer going to work the way it always had, I was suddenly struck by the realization that my life had changed permanently. Even if everything that doctors had done and continued to do worked out perfectly, the new Amberly Lago was not going to be like the old Amberly Lago.

I cried knowing I would never be able again to do the things I'd done my whole life. I cried that I couldn't run and play with my kids and husband and friends and grandchildren. I cried that I couldn't work. I cried at how angry I felt, and how tired I was of feeling tired and in pain. I cried over how much I cried. I cried because no words could express what I felt.

For quite a while that night, I wallowed in the unfairness of it all, even to the point of wondering what I might have done to deserve what'd happened. Thankfully, I got past that point quickly and back to the mystery of life, whether there's a grand plan—or God's Grand Plan—behind it all.

All you must do is read a single history book to know that, since the dawn of time, hundreds of millions (billions?) of innocents have suffered much crueler fates than the one I was facing. Bad things happen to good people, and good things happen to bad people.

But if you think about it, that randomness is what makes life interesting, intriguing, and worth living.

Imagine, for a moment, what life would be like if bad things happened only to bad people, and good people were instantly rewarded. Wouldn't that seem like an even more absurd existence? All the mystery, the not knowing what was going to happen from one moment to the next, would be removed. Which would be deadly boring and produce the opposite results from what we unthinkingly assume. Ask yourself: Who watches a ball game or a tennis match or a race when the outcome is already known?

Because there's no direct evidence of God's existence, people who believe that God exists, or that life has a purpose, are said to have faith. And that lack of direct evidence is what causes atheists and cynics to insist that God doesn't exist. But whether you or I believe or don't believe in God or life's purpose is irrelevant. As a matter of logic, we'd all be less happy about getting up every morning if there were indeed proof one way or another because the greatest mystery of all would be solved.

Of course, that doesn't mean we can't rail against the Fates when something bad befalls us, but it does mean that we benefit when we count our blessings often and expansively. On that night, I was as pissed as I get, maybe because this was the first time since the accident I'd allowed myself to think what that man had done—and why he hadn't done anything for me, one human being to another.

The sheets have to be changed because all the blood that drains from the skins grafts kept leaking through the bandages and onto the bed.

Staring at those bandages, unable to see the donor site, as it was referred to, I imagined some deep Grand Canyon-like gouge. *It looks like they took the whole front side, all the way up to my hip,* I wrote. And it hurt. That was recorded several times, as if to make the point more emphatic. *Just to barely touch it kills me. I feel like I take two steps forward and ten steps back.*

I remember that night, and remember thinking I'd ever been foolish to think positively. Which was, of course, a foolish thing to think.

———

June 23, 2010.

Finally, finally, finally, at about noon I started feeling better from my unpleasant experience, which is about the nicest way I can put it. I've had a pretty relaxing day, though I canceled the visits of two friends who were scheduled and whom I was looking forward to seeing. I just needed some down time, and I wasn't sure how crabby I was going to be.

Is there anyone who can endure such misery without being crabby? I don't know. I doubt it. But if I'm going to be in pain the rest of my life, which is apparently a possibility,

I'll have to be the first person to do so. I am not willing to be someone who my friends and family don't recognize because something they can't see—my pain—has changed who I am and why they like and love me. So whatever happens from here on out, I'm going to have to learn to accommodate it. And I will.

According to my blood work, my blood sugar was way up a few days ago. The doctor immediately wanted to put me on medication for it. I told him no. I said I'd bring it down myself. He begged me to go on meds. I said I was on enough meds. He said my blood sugar was dangerously high. I told him to take me off the dextrose bag in the IV and give me just saline. Reluctantly, he did. And in a day my sugar went from 161 to 108.

———

June 28, 2010.

They're preparing me to leave the hospital, which I'm tempted to say I'd give up my right leg to do, but never mind. In preparation, they're weaning me off the pain meds. I'm not nearly as drugged up, but my pain level is higher too.

The nurses have been angels. I honestly still don't understand how they do what they do every day, or every other day, for years at a time. It's a phenomenal thing to take care of people at their sickest and most helpless, when they're vulnerable and depressed and grouchy. All I have to do is push a button by my bed, and nurse shows up. God bless them all.

It's been exactly one month since the accident. Never did I think that I'd have been in the hospital that long, and I suppose if I'd lost my leg, I'd have been discharged long ago, with a prescription for occupational therapy as an out-patient every day.

I kept pressing Dr. Wiss on when I might be able to go

home, and he didn't take it well. He doesn't know, and made it clear he's not going to be rushed, not after all this work.

"My friend Sam is coming to see me tomorrow. We've talked on the phone a few times, and he's always so encouraging. He said we would race each other to the top of the hill, which is so sweet, but right now I can't even get my foot to a ninety-degree angle without crying in pain.

I wonder if some of what's going on in my body and brain is directly related to being weaned off the meds. Am I going through supervised withdrawal? Well, whatever it is, it doesn't change the fact that I'm so emotional. I can't stop crying. I'm scared. My head hurts. And no matter how many times I tell myself that it's going to be better, and I'm going to live a normal life again, it just doesn't feel that way right now. The other night I kept crying and crying when some friends called me from a party. All of them were together, and I could hear the music and laughter in the background, and it sounded like everyone was having so much fun. I wonder if I'll ever be able to have fun like that again.

————

June 30, 2010.

For a minute there, I thought I was going to get out of jail by tomorrow. They took me off my IV, which means no more pain pump. Wow. I'd gotten so used to it, I didn't realize just how much it was working. Once again, like all things, we don't truly appreciate what we have till it's gone. My pain now is just right at the edge of tolerable. If it stays like this, I'll be okay. Or I think I will.

Dr. [X] came in this afternoon to take out the drain that was embedded six inches into my leg, keeping the site clean. He was about to pull and I said, "Hang on, aren't you going to give me a topical or something before you do this?" He said, "Nah, you're tough, it'll be over in a second," and then he yanked. I think the man might be a sadist. It burned. And I didn't even have the pain pump to mask it. But then he cleaned all of my scabs, which looked pretty gross, before bandaging it up again.

"The most important thing I did all day was go outside. All by myself. I lifted myself out of bed and into the wheelchair, then wheeled myself out the door, down the hall, to the elevator, to the plaza level—which I could do because I'm no longer hooked up to any IV lines. YAY! The PT supervisor says I'm the only person on the floor who can do this.

I honestly can't remember ever feeling such freedom. It also helps prove my case that I deserve to get out of here. I ordered a wheelchair for the house, and Johnny ordered a hospital bed, so everything I'll have to do at home is what I can already do here. Any day now.

The doctors have no doubt how badly I want to leave here. I've made it infinitely clear to them, and also made it clear to everyone at the hospital how grateful I am for everything. But I'm so, so, so tired of being dependent on nurses and doctors. I can't get the thought out of my mind that being dependent on them is slowing my recovery, the same way that working a muscle builds it. Anyway, that's how it seems to me. Part of me thinks (not seriously, but maybe) that I'm being kept here because so many nurses come in just to hide out, or to tell me their problems and ask advice. Some of them end up telling me their whole life stories, and some want me to know they're keeping up with the exercise plans I wrote for them. It does make me feel good. The head nurse came in to tell me I should come back and teach a class.

———

July 1, 2010.

YES!!! They came in to tell me I can go home!!!!!!
It's been five weeks since the accident. What a ride
it's been, like the ultimate roller coaster. Ups and
downs and downs and ups, and just when I thought
I couldn't get any lower, I'd come up and think I was
there to say, then I'd drop lower than before. And like
a real roller coaster, there was plenty of screaming.
Getting my staples out and my leg wrapped didn't
hurt too much until one staple hit a nerve. I nearly
jumped through the roof. The nurse tried again, and
made me cry. So they ended up leaving it in and will
remove it next week.
The next test was proving I could walk on crutches.
OMG OMG OMG. Gravity is not my friend. All
the blood rushed down, and it felt like soldiers firing
weapons. The doctor had warned me, but there's
no way to prepare for something that bad. I could
stand it for only a few seconds, but my leg swelled
and turned purple, and afterward it felt like pins and
needles for about fifteen minutes. Actually, no, not
pins and needles—nails and screws, the nails being
hammered in, the screws being turned.
"What I can't get out of my mind is that this is just
the beginning of another journey.

I had no idea what kind of journey I was about to embark on.

28

James Dean

FROM AGE THIRTEEN, I'D BEEN ON my own financially, doing anything I could to make money for whatever I needed, primarily my dance lessons and saving for a car. I cleaned my dad's office, babysat, tutored math, and in high school began choreographing routines for the school's drill team at twenty-five bucks a pop. My friend Amy and I would make it up and split the money. I'd work out the steps and she'd write them down, and the whole process would take anywhere from thirty minutes to three hours, so however you calculated it, we did better than any minimum wage job—which I also got paid at a store at the mall called the Cookie Jar, where at sixteen I essentially ran the whole thing, from making the batter in those huge vats, to baking, to shelving them, to selling them, to cleaning up, and finally to counting the money and closing up. Eventually I convinced the owner to let me wear roller skates for efficiency, explaining how I could get from one place in the store to the others places I needed to be, which was always two places at once, a lot faster.

Working and dancing so much, I didn't have a lot of spare time. So not till I was seventeen did I have a boyfriend. Jack was six years older and a big deal in town, and was also considered the town rebel. Think James Dean. He came from a prominent family and was a good-looking man with charisma to burn. I was in elementary school when he was in high school and a lifeguard at the country club where everyone swam for a couple of bucks. That he was interested in me came as a shock and surprise, since at that point I still thought of myself as small and scrawny, having only recently become neither. I remembered how girls looked at him. On our first date, he grabbed my hips and said, "Yeah, I think these are child-bearing," which even then in my naiveté I understood to mean, "I want to have sex with you" (or words to that effect). One of my friends was dating one of his friends, and he suggested we all go out.

"With me?" I asked. "Really?"

He seemed like God's gift. On our first solo date, we were pulled over on a country road by the sheriff, not because he was speeding or doing anything wrong—he wasn't—but because the deputy wanted to have a close encounter with Jack. Anyway, it's not like he couldn't have gotten out of the ticket anyway. His uncle was a judge, and the family was a pretty big deal with lots of connections.

In time, when I knew I was going to be intimate with him, I decided I had to tell him about Mom's husband and what had happened—everything; the things he'd done, and the things he'd said. Unless all of it was out in the open ahead of time, I knew I'd be unable to go any further. That proved to be a wise decision. It's easier to knock down the wall than try to scale it.

29

Welcome Home

TO GET ME OUT OF THE hospital, Johnny had to arrange transportation. Jumping in his car, or anyone's car, wasn't feasible—not even in the backseat. At last he arranged for a special van and then arranged for occasional home nursing for me. I couldn't, after all, simply walk into the house and carry on; I had to have attendants to do for me for what I couldn't do for myself, and a nurse to administer antibiotics intravenously. The fear of osteomyelitis—a bone infection—was one of the major factors that had kept me in the hospital so long. My doctors wanted to be able to keep a constant vigil for any signs of infection that, in the hospital, could've been treated before advancing. Now, at home, experienced eyes would have to do that while also continuing to administer strong antibiotics through my picc line. Oh, and inject medicine into my belly to prevent blood clots. It would burn for a good five minutes each time. And that was on top of the ten different prescriptions that had to be taken at different times during the day.

The ride from my hospital bed to the van was in my new wheelchair, one that was going home with me, with a sheet tied to my leg to keep it from falling. I may as well have been running the gauntlet. Nurses, doctors, orderlies, candy stripers—everyone who'd ever had contact with me (and was on duty that day) came out to say goodbye. Many of them handed me cards, some that had been signed by everyone who knew I would be leaving and wasn't on duty that day. It took five times as long as it should have to reach the elevator, because of all the hugs and tears. I will remember those moments always.

As soon as we reached the van, its driver lowered a hydraulic lift and I was pushed into the back. The driver, a middle-aged man who probably had kids, berated me much of the way home for riding a motorcycle. It would've been funny if it was funny. Or appropriate. It was neither. The whole time I wished he would keep his thoughts to himself and drive in a way that smoothed out the bumps. My toes, I could see, were starting to swell, and my leg throbbed. At one point, he had to pull over so I could take my meds.

At last we pulled into my driveway. There was a huge banner over the front door that said WELCOME HOME, but my immediate thought was, *Oh, no, now people will come over to try to cheer me up, and I won't be able to pretend that I'm cheered up.*

Inside were a few dozen balloons and more welcome signs. I was wheeled into the family room, adjacent to the kitchen, where Johnny had removed all the furniture and arranged for a hospital bed to be set up—right next to a kind of portable toilet. I was bound and determined to use it as soon as possible instead of raising myself onto the bedpan for someone to empty. And I sure as heck wasn't going to wear a diaper that had to be changed. Right now, the possibility of wheeling myself across the room, then down a short hallway and into the powder room, was beyond imagination. As was getting up the stairs to where the bedrooms were.

Contemplating all that was a little disheartening.

In the first half hour, five people—friends and neighbors—dropped by. I'd gotten good at conveying gratitude for someone's thoughtfulness and yet also a tacit message that I was in no mood, which I wasn't after that painful ride and the shock of being home without it really feeling like being home—not the way "Ah, home sweet home" comes over you when you return from being out of town. I needed to accommodate myself to my surroundings without the intrusion of visitors looking at me like some kind of specimen, which of course they didn't intend to do. But it was natural. "I'm exhausted," I said, and they all got the hint.

Poor Johnny. He'd been three people for a month now, taking care of me, taking care of Ruby, arranging everything at the hospital and home—and yet still working his job.

I tried to get used to my new surroundings, which were familiar but seemed so new, and somehow sad, because I could no longer get up and walk over to the kitchen, or the living room, or climb the stairs. Those kinds of things were points of reference to reality, ones I'd missed for the previous month in the hospital. I was still a prisoner of bed, even if that bed was in my own home.

That night I slept reasonably well, probably because my house is a lot quieter than any hospital. At two, though, I had to wake up for bodily functions. I don't know how Johnny knew, because I was quiet and he was all the way upstairs, but he came running down to empty it for me. Bless him. What a thing to do in the middle of the night when you're sleeping. And then he did it again at 5:30, and this time made me some coffee, too, before going back to bed himself.

I sat there sipping my coffee, feeling anxious about the physical therapist who was going to be there in a few hours because I knew it was going to be torture. But most of all I felt grateful for my life, for my husband who would quite literally do anything for me, and for my little girl, who any minute now was going to wake up and come running down the stairs and jump in bed with me. Between them and Savanna, I was motivated to do anything and everything it would take to get stronger.

Of course, at that moment, I couldn't imagine how much I was about to hurt.

30

Salt Shakers and Smoke

ALL THROUGHOUT SCHOOL, I'D BEEN ACTIVE in student government. It was important to me in ways I wouldn't have known how to explain at the time, and I'm not sure even today if I did it because I wanted to excel in any way I could, or because staying busy was another way to have an excuse not to be anywhere near Mom's husband.

Of course, there were also perks that went with being on student council. One of them was an annual road trip to Austin, Texas. In the eighth grade, I'd gotten to go with a teacher and a few other council members to Austin, the state capital, and for whatever reason I remember only one thing about that trip. Here I was, in this historic city—a place I'd never been—and what's still stuck in my memory is going to a restaurant there with Mrs. G, as I'll call her, and watch her blithely, unashamedly, openly steal the salt and pepper shakers off the table.

"I like these," she said with a smile as she stuffed them in her purse. That wasn't the sort of thing she would ever have done back home in Greenville, where everyone knew everyone, even if there'd been more than a few restaurants in Greenville. (It was a big deal when the McDonald's opened in town.) I never again looked at her in the same way, and from then on, I never didn't notice that she smelled like cigarettes.

It's funny that that sort of familiarity with everyone in Greenville was both one of the best things about growing up there, and something I couldn't wait to leave behind as I planned my move to California after high school. In Greenville, everybody knew everybody, and there was no such thing as anonymity in affairs of the heart or even affairs of the pocketbook. In California, I knew I'd be able to go into a store and buy what it was I went there for without the clerk or owner knowing who I was and possibly telling someone else for whatever reason ("Oh, Amberly must have her period. I wonder if Jack knows."). Poor celebrities, having to endure being recognized everywhere, and have everything they say, do, and wear end up online, in magazines, or on TV. No wonder they go to such lengths sometimes to disguise themselves.

In retrospect, I think there was something useful about having grown up in that environment. It allowed you to see people for who they really are, not who they pretend to be, even if everyone was pretending to be God-fearing and enviable. Greenville was not a place that nurtured romantics, and I very much appreciate that. Same as I appreciate having learned to work for what I want and rely on myself.

31

Progress, not Perfection

THE PHYSICAL THERAPIST'S NAME WAS DARIA, and it was clear from the first moment that she'd never seen an injury as grotesque as mine. She spent a minute or two looking at it, trying to keep her poker face, but she wasn't very good at it.

She asked for the X-rays. Johnny had laid them on the table. She held them against the sliding glass door where the sun was coming in, as if it were a light box, and shook her head. I wondered if she was going to throw up, though at that point I didn't know if it was for her or for me—that is, the task she had ahead of her.

"I've never seen or worked with anything this complicated," she said. "Okay, go ahead and raise your leg off the bed a couple of inches."

For the previous weeks, I'd been able to use my upper body strength to lift my body onto the bedpan, but I'd never tried to lift my leg by itself while still on my bed. When the bandages needed changing, two nurses had been required, one to lift my leg and one to do the bandaging. So, I hadn't tried since the day I swung my leg over the motorcycle and rode away from gym.

Now I tried and couldn't do it. It was as if I'd been paralyzed, though of course the pain said very loudly that I hadn't been. And yet there was a disconnect between my brain that I was telling to do something and its ability to carry out my orders.

I looked at her with what must have been terror in my eyes, wondering if I'd ever again be able to move my leg.

"Don't panic," she said, "you'll get there."

Really? If she could see panic in my eyes, I could see concern in hers, enough to question whether she believed what she was telling me. I kept trying, and kept getting the same result.

But Daria wasn't done. First, she massaged and manipulated my hip that had gotten so tight over the weeks. That felt good. Then she helped me to maneuver to the side of the bed and helped me to stand on the good leg with the bad one hanging down. Or try to.

The past month had been thirty days of pain that varied in intensity according to what was being done, all the way back to the moment of the accident and the doctor trying to clamp off my femoral artery. But until now, everything that felt like pain from the Spanish Inquisition had to do with people touching me to do this or that. Other than Daria's helping me to pivot to the side of the bed, that wasn't the case here.

Oh.

My.

God.

The blood rushed so fast into my leg, thanks to gravity, it felt like it would explode. I could only suck it up for a few seconds, after which I collapsed back on the bed. That, along with not being able to lift my leg, I almost wished I hadn't left the hospital and began wondering whether any of this would ever work. My eyes filled with tears and I asked Daria, "Is it normal to cry during physical therapy?"

She assured me we'd get through this together, and promised we wouldn't do that again for a while. But at the moment I didn't believe we'd get through this. It took my leg a good fifteen minutes to get back to its normal level of agony, and I emphasized that I didn't want to do that again until I could at least lift my legs off the bed.

When she left, I tried several times to lift, figuring that standing had reinvigorated the neural pathways. But still, nothing happened. I was exhausted, slept much of the day, then all the way through the night, waking at six-thirty with the feeling that elves had broken into the house and dropped cinderblocks on me. How could everything hurt? Every part of my body? I actually wondered whether I was having a nightmare about hurting. But no, it was real.

A couple of hours later Daria showed up, and we repeated the first day's activities with the same result—and after she left I tried a number of times to do leg lifts. By the third or fourth day, I was getting increasingly panicked, though at least I was able to take the pain of my leg being down for a full fifteen seconds. So that counted as progress, I told myself—always looking for some good news to hang onto.

Finally, after about a week, the signal started to get through. I could tell it was going to work even before it did. In fact, I kind of announced it after five or six failed tries. There was a moment when something seemed to be happening in my leg, something barely perceptible but noticeable nonetheless. It was as though the road crew came with a backhoe and moved the last bit of dirt from the highway that had fallen during the landslide, and with the obstacle cleared, cars could pass. I'm being overly metaphoric, but really, there was a kind of strange sensation which made me say, "Okay, watch."

Then I did it. My leg rose several inches off the bed, and I held it there before lowering it. Johnny was there, watching, and—I could tell—holding back tears. Because if you think about it, he couldn't have known—not for sure—that something hadn't happened permanently to me. So, any sign that I wasn't paralyzed had to have affected him. I never feared that Johnny feared being married to a one-legged woman; that wasn't the reason he'd worked so hard to save my leg. Nor did I fear what he'd do if I never progressed beyond this point. He loved me, of that I was sure, and the comfort that that knowledge gave me was like a cocoon.

I didn't even mind the significant pain because now I knew that I could—and would—get to the next step, then the one after that. It occurred to me that not being able to move my leg was my body's (well, my brain's) way of protecting it, like when I'd had that car accident at sixteen and told the paramedics I was fine. Well, no, I wasn't fine, as I proved when my leg wouldn't move and I collapsed on the ground. "Can you move it?" doctors ask when you hurt yourself, because moving it or not being able to are huge clues to what's going on.

Clearly, I was still far from being able to get myself into a wheelchair or onto crutches. The majority of time I still had to lie on my back. It was so bad that I got bedsores on my right heel, pelvis, and shoulder from lying in the same place for so long. Bedsores are a big deal. Older people confined to beds for a long time get them relatively quickly and, if they're not noticed and treated promptly—which can be hard to do—often lead to deadly systemic infections. On one day, I had to spend three straight hours, with Daria, trying to figure out how to find what posture I should lie in most of the time, and how to bring down the swelling in my foot—and when I say swelling, I'm talking about blow-up-doll kind of swelling—without aggravating the sores. In the end, we constructed a tower of pillows that elevated my leg a foot above my bed.

But I couldn't stay like that all the time, so we made several changes, one of which was to order a special mattress and sheets that were recommended by the nurses to prevent bedsores. Then I learned to sleep propped up on my side, which was more or less like trying to take a nap in a difficult yoga pose.

All of these were painful, annoying, dismaying inconveniences that I could live with as long as I knew I was improving, even if only incrementally. And slowly. For whatever reason—actually, it was the reason that had led me to train several clients, do a full workout, and run eleven miles in a personal-best time the day of my accident—what I found hardest to endure at the time was my nearly complete loss of muscle mass.

Doing nothing had made my muscles melt away. All of the hard work I'd put in over the years—the sweaty, straining work that enabled me to good-naturedly embarrass macho men in the weight room who'd smirked and chuckled at a "girl" being in there with them; the groaning, achy work that enabled me to hold my own against my big strong husband—those muscles had atrophied to near nothingness. Pretty much I felt like a bunch of bones lying inert in a sack, and it upset me in a way that's hard to defend, considering how many other issues I was facing.

32

I'll Be in California

JACK HAD ENROLLED IN LAW SCHOOL in Texas, and I was getting ready to leave for California, which was what I'd repeatedly made clear I intended to do at more or less the exact moment I got my diploma. While everyone else I knew was making plans for the summer, I was deciding which clothes I would stuff into the back of the little Suzuki I'd bought, and trying to earn more money that I could add to the $1200 I'd already saved. With a goal of finally ending up in Los Angeles, I figured it was wise to first get out to California in general any way I could, especially because I had limited funds and knew no one in L.A.

"At least I'll be in California," I kept saying.

So, I arranged to stay for a while with my second cousin, Al, and his wife, who lived in one of the cities in the East Bay of the San Francisco Bay Area. They knew to expect me a week or so after graduation.

My friend Dan said he'd accompany me, so I wouldn't have to drive all that way—two long days sandwiched around a short night of sleep in a motel—by myself. Being that I was still absurdly naïve about males and their intentions, because I frankly still didn't believe that any of them found me attractive, I didn't realize that my "friend" Dan might have had other ideas than carpooling. But Jack did. He said, "No way is he going out there with you. I am." He wanted to keep me company to keep me from keeping company with anyone else.

At the time, Jack was due to start law school at Texas Tech, in Lubbock, a month or two later. But he drove out there with me, and I was glad he was there, especially when the car broke down in Albuquerque. Fortunately, it was a part that was subject to a recall, so it didn't cost me anything. We took our time, traveling only a couple of hundred miles a day, staying in the cheapest motels we could find and eating McDonald's. The best part of the trip was stopping at the Grand Canyon.

When we got to California, Jack stayed only a few days more before he had to return to Texas. And I needed to be on my own to the degree I could.

At first I did some cooking and cleaning for my cousins in exchange for my room and board, but then we decided that I'd move into their basement apartment and pay rent. They were so sweet, they didn't charge as much as they would have otherwise if I were a tenant. Right away I opened the Yellow Pages and started cold calling dance studios in the area, identifying myself as a professional dance teacher. One woman invited me to stop by her studio. I did, and after we talked a few minutes she said, "Let me have you teach this next class"—which was jazz—as a kind of audition. I was nervous, of course, since it had happened so fast and so unexpectedly, but I remembered all the dues I'd been paying as a dance teacher since age thirteen. I must've done pretty well because I was hired to teach classes at not only that studio but also two others in the area that she managed.

Then my dream came true and I landed my first gig

dancing in a music video for M. C. Hammer, who lived up the road in Oakland. This kind of thing was what I'd come to California for, and I was ecstatic. This gave me hope that when I got to L.A. I'd be working all the time as a dancer.

I also began modeling for various photographers who did stock photography and catalogs. And I kept the cash coming in, even on days I didn't have gigs, by waiting tables in an Oakland two-story restaurant where, if you got the upstairs section—which I usually did as the youngest, tallest, and strongest waitperson—you had to balance multiple plates on both arms as you went up and down eighteen steps; no trays allowed. It was quite a workout. That's how I thought about it, as a workout without working out. To me, it was all about mindset.

There wasn't a day when I didn't work one job or another because it was clear to me that my dreams weren't going to come true by magic. I'd have to work for them, and save for them. No one was going to stop me on the street and hand me a wad of cash with best wishes for a nice life. No leprechaun was going to lead me to a pot of gold at the end of the rainbow. In fact, neither of my parents was going to come out to California, help me find the ideal apartment, take me to Ikea for some furniture, and slip an envelope of mad money into my purse to get me started. I was on my own, and I wouldn't have had it any other way, because my success would be solely and wholly mine.

One day Jack called and said he hated law school in Texas, and had applied to a law school in San Francisco—a very good law school, I later heard. How he applied and was admitted so quickly after dropping out of a law school he'd already begun, I don't know, but he was supposed to start in the winter semester. I told him I was still planning to go to L.A. not long after that, but he came out anyway and we moved into a tiny apartment together in Alameda, near the naval base.

We didn't stay for very long, though. One day I told Jack I was going to spend the following month in Los Angeles, prepping for the auditions at the dance school where I was hoping to get a scholarship, the Joe Tremaine Dance Center in North Hollywood. It was considered one of the best dance schools in the country, the place where casting directors always checked out the talent for their productions. If I didn't get a scholarship, I wasn't sure I could work enough hours to pay for room and board along with school too. Because even if I didn't win a scholarship, I was determined to enroll for the following year. And since I didn't plan on sleeping on the street or eating water sandwiches for dinner, getting that scholarship was critical. My plan was to go down there and take several classes a day—paying for them, of course— so that I could get a feel for the place and let the teachers see me. Not only would I have my feet wet, they'd recognize me as someone willing to work harder than anyone else and, hopefully, believe that I had the talent.

It worked. They granted me and a few others a scholarship and gave us two weeks to get everything in order before classes began. I couldn't remember being happier, and as I drove back to pick up my stuff my cloud nine was dampened only by knowing how hard Jack was going to take it.

I wasn't wrong. Here he was in the middle of his first semester of law school, which didn't give him a lot of time to do anything but study, and now he was having to deal with losing me in the middle of torts. I felt bad but not guilty. After all, I'd told him before he came out that I planned to leave. Maybe he hadn't believed me. Maybe he'd thought I would stick around once he got out here, that I would be overwhelmed, that I'd realize he was my soul mate; that I'd wait while he became a lawyer; that we'd get married, I'd have all those babies he told me on our first date I was going to have, and together the five or eight of us would live happily ever after.

If so, that had been a serious miscalculation, one born of not knowing me well enough or not paying attention to what I'd made clear about my intentions or not believing that this little girl he remembered from his days as a lifeguard really, wanted what she claimed to want.

Or maybe he was so used to girls who'd tell Jack anything they thought he wanted to hear to be the wife who gave him all those children. Whatever the truth was for him, I would not let anything get in the way of going after what I wanted. I'd come too far to get sidetracked by love. Nothing short of death was going to stop me from giving it my best. I'd sucked up far too much myself to have nothing to show for it. Even so, I didn't like seeing him hurt.

33

This Fine Man

DURING THE FIRST WEEK THAT JOHNNY was back at work, he hired a woman to stay with me and make me food or do whatever else I needed. But I didn't like her being there, mostly because I felt like a burden and wanted to be able to care for myself. After that I stayed by myself, except for Daria's physical therapy visits and the drop-in nurses who checked on me and administered shots, until he took off work early in the afternoon to pick up Ruby from daycare at three o'clock.

By the second week, Johnny could see I needed a break. He lifted me into the wheelchair and rolled me outside, my first time out since I'd been home. Tears filled my eyes, not because I was outside, though I was glad to be, but because of Johnny. I felt so grateful that our paths had crossed and he'd become my husband. The day before, on July 4th, he could've gone out to a barbecue down the block with a bunch of our friends; I urged him to, because he needed to have some fun, none of which he'd had since the accident. But on his day off, he wouldn't leave my side, same as the way after work he thought only and entirely of making sure my needs were met, the needs I couldn't meet myself, including running to the place a mile away for my favorite oatmeal, or making me coffee first thing in the morning (or, of course, emptying my bed pan without complaint—though usually with a joke). There was nothing he wouldn't, or didn't, do for me, and I thanked heaven for bringing us together. That's how I felt. I felt that all my years of sucking it up and putting one foot in front of the other (which at the time was a funny phrase to me) when I thought the world was caving in, had rewarded me with this fine man.

"What's wrong?" he said, seeing my tears.

"You."

"Me? What did I do?"

"Everything."

That was the truth. If it weren't for him, I'd now be learning to get around on one leg. If it weren't for him, I'd have had to hire someone like him to take care of all that needed taking care of, and no one could have done that at any price.

34
The Best of Them

I MOVED INTO AN L.A. APARTMENT not far from the school with another dance student I'd met the previous month. We'd both needed a place, both needed to save money, and both wanted to have only a short drive to school in that crazy traffic.

The classes offered were jazz, ballet, tap, modern, and hip-hop. I took them all. Most classes lasted ninety minutes. Most days I took five classes, though a few times I took eight, which I agree was foolish. It didn't take long before I ditched the ballet classes because I was too tall for ballet; there were no partners to match up with. In fact, at five eleven I was almost too tall to be a dancer at all, at least a background dancer. We'd have scholarship shows attended by all the biggest agents and casting directors, and while I may have been able to book gigs based on my talent and skill and looks, I know there were many I didn't get—especially going on tours with artists—because you don't want the girl in the back row to be taller than the star or in any way make the star look shorter.

Besides casting directors, booking agents would come to the shows, too, looking for clients. There were three main dance agencies in the business, according to what I'd read and heard, and also from what I could see. I wanted to be associated with the best of them, and as long as all three were interested in me, I could have my pick. So, who was best?

Well, more people said, "Oh, you have to go with Julie Erickson" than they did the other two. But I wasn't going to sign with anyone I didn't have a personal connection with, which was why I sat down and interviewed—well, talked to— the heads of all three. As it happened, I did have the strongest connection with Erickson, who, as it also happened, booked models too.

The more I danced, the more I loved it. The more classes I took, the better I got. The better I got, the more jobs I booked. The more jobs I booked, the more classes I took because no matter how good you are, you're never going to get even better—and you can *always* get better—unless you keep practicing and learning. I was booking enough jobs to make not only more money than I'd ever made, but more money than I had even anticipated making at this point. I was young, single, and loving life.

Yet as much I loved dancing and the life it afforded, I could already see by the fourth or fifth professional gig that this wasn't what I wanted to be doing after age twenty-five. Professional baseball, basketball, and football players might be able to extend their careers into their late thirties and forties (though the wear and tear on their bodies in those sports is more extreme than most of what a dancer endures). But those professional athletes know they're the best of the best, earn millions or tens of millions a year, and their longevity is a testament to having reached the pinnacle of their respective professions. There's nothing higher than Major League Baseball, the National Football League, and the National Basketball Association. Dancers, though, have nothing unambiguously equivalent. Even on the New York stage or Bolshoi Ballet, at twenty-five you're likely to be outbooked by younger dancers. We're talking about women and women's bodies and what society—both men and women—admire about the female form. It's cruel, it's heartless, it's not fair, and there's nothing to be done about it. Things are the way they are, and howling at the moon doesn't change any of it.

35
Endless Possibilities

THERE WAS A BIG DIFFERENCE BETWEEN being in the hospital and being at home. I'd gotten used to having nurses and orderlies empty the bedpan in the hospital, but I could tell I was never going to get used to someone emptying it at home. I mean, I didn't want Johnny to be saddled with this extremely unpleasant deed, and I was certain he would shout for joy the day he no longer had to, but I could reconcile his doing it with my own embarrassment at needing it done in a way I couldn't with anyone else, even if they were getting paid for doing the job. What I had to accept was that it would be a very long time—months? year? years?—before I was able to go upstairs and sleep in my own bed and use my own bathroom.

In those early days, I openly questioned how much of my previous life I was going to be able to live again. I knew what I wanted to happen, but not even the doctors knew what was possible. After all, the very first doctor had said he'd never seen more damage to a leg outside of a war zone. This was all uncharted territory, and the only certainty was my own will. Which meant anything the doctors said short of telling me I'd soon be able to do what I wanted was irrelevant anyway.

At that time, my will, my desire was to relieve myself of the embarrassment of having to use a bedpan, and relieve Johnny of having to empty the bedpan, by relieving myself in the downstairs bathroom thirty feet away. How badly I wanted to do that can be described only by a crude analogy that literally everyone can relate to: How badly do you *really* want to find a bathroom when you're out in public and you *really* have to go, and you think you're maybe five seconds away from soiling yourself? Well, that's how badly I wanted to use my downstairs powder room by myself.

That said, it wasn't something that could be easily managed. Yes, I could've made it to the door of the powder room (toilet and sink) in a wheelchair, my leg extended, as it had been every time I'd been in a wheelchair since the accident. But then what? The door was too narrow for the wheelchair, and even if we'd had it widened, it would've taken a complete remodeling of the space inside to accommodate the chair. Which might have been something we'd have attempted, at exorbitant cost, if doing so could conceivably have solved the problem. But it couldn't have. Because I was still going to have to get from the wheelchair to the toilet (using upper-body strength), and keep my legs down while sitting on the toilet.

At the risk of seeming too graphic (though by now there's not much left to hide), ask yourself how hard you imagine it would be to relieve yourself when you're in so much pain you can't think straight. Well, that's what it would've entailed. So why bother with the bathroom remodel (using money we didn't have anyway, with hospital bills approaching seven figures) when it would've still left me in the same situation: unable to use the toilet.

No, what it was going to take for me to use that powder room was to enter under my own body's power—not by walking, per se, because that wouldn't be for a long, long time, if ever.

It was going to be by crutches. Crutches, more than a wheelchair, were going to afford me the kind of locomotion that I could live with and feel jazzed about. In a wheelchair, you're a passenger, and someone else might be driving. In fact, even if you're rolling yourself, it's the wheels doing the work. The Sumerians, bless them, invented the wheel and changed all of human history. There'd have been no progress without the wheel. But I could never get past the sense—because I didn't want to get past the sense, and believed that if I had accommodated myself to the sense of knowing that I could always fall back on the wheel—that accepting any alternative to the goal I was aiming for would prevent me from reaching that goal.

Crutches are a form of walking. You see people on the kind of crutches that look permanent and imagine how hard it would be to have to move like that all the time. Imagining it is easy, especially if, like many people, you've had to walk on crutches for any period of time. Even if you haven't, the mechanism of using your arms to place a fulcrum down on the ground ahead of you and swing one or both legs forward is not beyond imagination.

Of course, to use crutches, you have to keep your legs pointed down and put weight on one of them. I calculated that to swing my legs over the side of the bed, grab the crutches, lift myself, and make it to the door, then maneuver my way into the bathroom, and, because of where the toilet is located—behind the open door—wiggle backward after closing it, followed by sitting and doing what needed doing, all while my leg was either down or resting on one of the crutches would take, at minimum, three minutes. Then that would be followed by an arduous return trip (including getting around the door) made more arduous by the vicious and rising pain level. In all I'd need at least four minutes of having my leg and blood flow at the mercy of gravity. And at that time the best I could manage was a few seconds.

In a way, I appreciated having a specific goal—to get to the bathroom—instead of just, "Oh, I want to be better." It gave me an opportunity to approach this methodically, doing it for however long I could stand it, then lying back down and elevating my leg until the worst of the pain passed—usually fifteen minutes—then getting up and trying again, hanging tough at least one second longer than the previous time.

So that's how it went, with me gutting out the feeling of my leg about to explode while being devoured by fire ants for five seconds—counting aloud, one one-thousand, two one-thousand, three one-thousand—then eight seconds, then fifteen seconds, and so on. My leg's nerves were apparently so out of whack that when the blood rushed in, they began firing crazily. After each time, I collapsed back on the bed and elevated my leg (lifting it myself under the thigh).

As odd as it sounds, there was something mystical about accepting the pain as a given, trying to suck it up, and being bigger than it. In high school, we studied how some American Indian tribes would purposely inflict pain on themselves to cleanse or purify them of bad spirits, which I understood to mean sins. In fact, there was a movie about fifty years ago called *A Man Called Horse*, which I believe was based on the true story of an Englishman in the nineteenth century who joined or was captured by the Sioux, and as either punishment or initiation was subjected to a grotesque torture intended to test him. For me, the test was to see whether I could live with what I began calling my new normal.

As should be evident by now, I use anything to motivate myself to achieve whatever goal I've set. Every time I stood, I lasted a little bit longer, and insisted on taking less recovery time. In a way, it began to seem like some sort of weight training exercise: three sets of eight reps—or something like that.

There was no way out of this but through, and no one could do it for me. My leg was my leg was my leg, and if I wanted to use it again, I'd have to push through and push myself into shape, almost exactly the way you go from a hundred pounds overweight to lean and fit. There's no pill, no shortcut, no proxy. You just do it, day by day, hour by hour, minute by minute. My goal was to have a life (which fittingly, I decided, began with using the toilet by myself), so I had no other choice.

An entry from my journal dated early July sums up what I knew I was up against:

> *I am going to do my exercises in a minute, and I'm trying to psyche myself up. I have never felt such pain before. I feel like I can't move. Then I cry and get frustrated. Frustrated and angry at the situation I am in. Angry that I am stuck in this bed. Angry at my leg that isn't working the way it has always worked for me in the past. I am facing one of my biggest challenges. Patience. I don't want to lose faith. Then I'm done crying and I remember that this too shall pass. This whole process is going to be two steps forward, three steps back, four steps forward, five steps back, until one day I'm taking more steps forward than backward. I don't know when that day will be, but if I don't take the steps, it'll be never. That's the story of everything, I suppose. I wonder if Michelangelo felt like that along about the third year of painting the Sistine Chapel. One brush stroke at a time. One brush stroke at a time.*

36
Long Enough

IN LOS ANGELES AND NEW YORK and other entertainment towns, one of the reasons so many of the waiters and waitresses at restaurants are aspiring performers—actors, dancers, etc.—is that restaurant work hours are generally at night (though of course there's a lunch shift too), freeing the staff for auditions during the day; and if there's something you do have to do, you can always find someone with the day off who'd be happy to pick up your shift. And when you do get a real gig that allows you to quit the restaurant—and it doesn't turn out to be your big break—you can usually get rehired by that restaurant when there's an opening, or move to somewhere else. Also, waiting tables is a good way to keep cash in your pocket.

In any event, I worked at a few restaurants in Los Angeles while I was dancing. I never wanted to be without work, even when I was booking a lot of dancing gigs. One of the first jobs I got in L.A. amazes me to this day. I went into the mall in Century City, which back then was still one of highest-end retail spots in town, and walked door-to-door asking if they needed anyone, regardless of what the establishment was.

The first place that said yes was a jewelry store run by an old man who never even asked for references or work history. Which is pretty odd, considering the value of what I had access to. I suppose he knew an honest face when he saw it, because it wasn't long before he began trusting me to open and close the store and make deliveries of both cash and jewels. The amount of trust he had in me was touching, even humbling, and I almost felt bad leaving for a job where I could make more money—Houston's, the restaurant.

I liked the job and the people and the hours. What I didn't like was the location, in Century City. One day when I came out of an audition, I saw a place called the California Canteen. It was located on Cahuenga, between the studios in Burbank and Hollywood proper—a great area for people, places, and things, and centrally located to almost every- where I'd ever need to be. So, I ran in, as much to get out of the rain as anything. By luck, the owner was there. I asked if there were any job openings. In a French accent he said, "Can you start tomorrow?"

I said sure. He said, "Good; see you tomorrow."

I drove home and realized that I'd been so excited to land the job, I'd forgotten to ask some truly important questions. I had no idea what job I'd been hired for or what to wear. Turns out I'd been hired as a bartender and was supposed to wear a white shirt with black jeans. Oh, and the California Canteen? It was a Basque restaurant. And all of the employees, except me, were either French or Basque. It didn't seem to matter to the bustling clientele that the bar didn't have spirits, only beer and wine. They loved the place. It was crowded all the time, and was frequented by a ton of celebrities, like Al Pacino and the cast of *Friends*. I loved working there except for being the odd-man-out. Two years of high school French were enough for me to know when the other employees were talking smack about me. Not that it mattered. It was a great job. And it was steady work.

My next job was waitressing at a nightclub restaurant called the Baked Potato. It's kind of famous for being the place to hear great jazz. A lot of polls list it as the top place in the area for jazz, and nearly every jazz musician, or any musician close to jazz, has played the Baked Potato. Probably more than once. Anytime sessions players or out-of-towners were around, they'd stop by and often sit in late at night. You never knew who was going to show, and that's part of what gave the Baked Potato its mystique and allure.

This is where I met my oldest daughter's father, who was a bartender at the nightclub. Right from the beginning, he wanted to date me, but I kept putting him off.

I'd tell him, "No, I've got a fiancé," referring to Jack, though it was obvious that Jack and I were going nowhere, especially since we weren't even in the same city.

But he kept pursuing me. I finally said yes because Jack and I weren't working out long distance.

I'll leave out a bunch of details, cut to the chase, and tell you that he and I were married only long enough to get my wonderful daughter Savanna out of the deal, which is why I don't regret the relationship.

37

On the Dash

I DON'T LIKE WRITING ABOUT MY pain, and I certainly imagine there's only a certain amount of it you can take reading about it. So, I won't be going on about it much more, at least not in detail. In deference to tedium and mindful that this isn't a medical textbook, I'll skip a number of things that at the time were consequential, events that would probably be among the most memorable happenings of most people's lives. But this *is* a book about having the life you imagine for yourself, even if circumstances have changed what's possible in reality. Always, always, always, your obligation to yourself is to imagine the best possible outcome under those circumstances and do everything it takes to make your imagination a reality. To that end, I'm obliged to lead you through a bit more pain as a way of dramatizing what's possible when you choose that reality as opposed to the reality you believe is being foisted on you.

Five days a week, Daria came over to work with me. The work was never pleasant. Never. The big milestone came when I was capable of walking on crutches to the bathroom, hopped backward into it, closed the door, and laid my bad leg up on the stool I used when showering. (I've neglected to wax poetic about the joys of showering—feeling hot water pouring down upon me and washing my own hair—after months of sponge baths and washings in the sink. It was the greatest of joys.)

A nurse arrived every day at about the same time to change my bandages. What I didn't know at the time was this reflected the doctors' fear that, even after sending me home from the hospital, I'd suffer a bone infection. No one, apparently, could believe that I'd made it out of the hospital, where infections are rampant, without developing the kind of bone infection that requires intravenous antibiotics for an extended period, though there was no guarantee they'd work to cure the osteomyelitis, which if it couldn't be—and osteomyelitis is often stubbornly resistant—would destroy the bone and require, yes, amputation. So, they were determined not to let all that good luck go to waste. Strangely, though, not until I called their attention to the bed sores on my heels and tailbone did they take them as seriously and treat them (with sterile gauze, antibiotic cream, and Vaseline) as seriously as my leg. Bed sores are a big deal. Older people who get them, and people in comas, can die quickly from infected sores.

One day a nurse came out from the defendant's insurance company to assess, or guesstimate, what it might cost me for a lifetime of medical supplies, care giving, and professional attention. They did one cost in case of an amputation, and one cost in case I saved my leg. She asked, "Can I look at your leg?"

"Sure," I said.

At the time, I was wearing two of the tightest-fitting compression socks. If I didn't, my leg would swell up like the Stay Puff Marshmallow Man in *Ghostbusters*. I lifted my pant leg up and started rolling the socks down. When she saw my leg, she said without emotion, as if my leg were a coffee table damaged in an earthquake, "So, are you going to keep it?"

I said, "What do you mean, 'am I going to keep it?' I kept it."

It was a chilling moment.

I'd like to say that it incited me further, but I'd already made up my mind that I was going to die with this leg, so my takeaway was to redouble my efforts.

The following day, or maybe two days later, I asked Daria to do something a little differently with me when she showed up. I said, "I need you to go out with me because I have to learn how to drive using only my left foot."

Against her better judgment and protesting the whole way, she drove me to an empty parking lot near the gym where I worked. We traded places. With my right leg up on the dash, I drove a few times around forward, then drove in reverse, then pulled into and out of imaginary parking places.

"Okay," I said, "I've got this. I'm good," and drove us home, with Daria white knuckling it all the way, I'm sure. That was a big deal for me.

By mid-August, a month after I got home, I could sneak out one day, get into my truck, put my right leg up on the dash, drive to the store, and pick out a birthday card for Johnny. That was an even bigger deal.

My first long walk, on crutches, was to the Starbucks in the small strip mall about two hundred yards away on the main drag, and it became the benchmark that I could measure my progress against. The hard part wasn't the upper-body strength needed to walk on crutches. The hard part was walking as fast as I could on the crutches so that my leg was pointed downward as little as possible.

About sixty yards from my front door, I took a seat on the short cinderblock wall the marks off a parking area, and raised my leg to rest a while and let the pain subside. When it did, I carried on, but had to take two more rests along the way to my destination—and of course the same on the way back. This walk that took fifteen minutes, including pauses, was something I used to do, sprinting, in about thirty seconds. So that was a little depressing. On the other hand, it was an accomplishment that only a week earlier had seemed impossible. So that's what I focused on. Focusing on what I'd lost rather than gained could've taken the heart out of me.

If the weather was warm, I'd put on shorts and a sleeveless tee, something that a lot of people—especially young women—wouldn't have done in my position. Which is to say that my leg was so atrophied, and the wound and scars so grotesque, I looked exactly like the accident victim I was. Plus, I still had the picc line in. For this former model, dancer, and fitness instructor, whose living used to depend on looking good and being fit, it was funny not to care a bit that people were gawking; some of them even commenting aloud. In my mind, this was like going into a storm cellar before the storm, having the cyclone destroy the neighborhood, then emerging afterward and saying, "Wow, what a beautiful day." I'd been inside too long, and had come too far, to care whether the sight of my leg made anyone uncomfortable.

To this day, that liberation from worry about what others might be thinking about me is one of the finest of the accident's ironic benefits. But it wasn't always like that. My perspective changed on a day when it was totally unexpected. I had gone in to see Dr. Wiss to get the results of another X-ray to see if the non-union of my tibia was slowly growing together. I would find out on this day if I needed a surgery to take a bone from my pelvis and transplant it to my leg to stimulate the bone to grow. I was looking down at my leg and hated it. I hated the scars and was angry at my leg for no longer doing what I wanted it to do.

At one point in time, I even asked one of my doctors that if they cut it off, would I be out of pain. The answer was no. Dr. Wiss came into the room and sat down right in front of me. He took my leg and gently placed it in his lap, right on his crisp, clean white coat. He held my leg as he examined it and looked at it as if were the most beautiful piece of art, his masterpiece. My eyes filled with tears. How could I hate something he viewed so beautiful? This leg was a miracle and from that day forward my entire perspective began to shift. I began to accept my new normal and really love my leg again.

In terms of progress milestones, the nearest and dearest to my heart, at least in memory, isn't using the toilet and shower by myself, or driving, or walking to Starbucks. It's going upstairs, lying on my own bed, and picking out something to wear from my closet. I'd pushed myself on my butt backward up the stairs before climbing up on my crutches (thanks to Johnny, who brought them up). My own bedroom, my own closet, were like dear old friends, and boy was I grateful to see them. True, none of my clothes fit; I'd lost so much weight. But I chose something myself, let it hang on me like a curtain, and vowed to never again complain about having nothing to wear.

38
Titanium

I WAS DOING WHAT THE DOCTOR told me to do. He said go ahead and do everything I was capable of doing. Because he'd told me I could and should bear weight on the bad leg, you'd better believe I took him at his word.

Of course, if you tell a normal person who'd had the kind of traumatic injury I'd had that she can bear weight on a leg that had only recently been bone confetti and was now being held together with titanium plates and screws, she probably doesn't interpret that to mean she can go back to the gym, ride the bike, lift weights—that is to say, return to her regular life as a gym rat. A normal person listens to her body's pain signals that were screaming louder than a fire alarm. Yes, she pushes through to a degree, knowing that not to do so means she'll never get better. But she doesn't pretend that worsening pain should be ignored. And that's what I did. Big mistake.

My grandfather had died, so I flew to Texas for the funeral and to commiserate with my family. Mom and my sister picked me up in Dallas. Before driving home, we stopped at the store to get some groceries. Wanting so badly to be normal, I left my crutches in the car and walked from there into the store. For a while I said nothing and pretended not to be silently screaming with every step, but after making it to only the front of the store, I told them I couldn't walk any further; either they needed to get me a wheelchair or fetch my crutches.

Worse than the pain, in a way, was the visual of what my leg did every time it touched the ground: it bowed out where it should've been straight. Think of Gumby. That was my leg. It was grotesque, and seemed to only be getting more deformed.

But did I think of going to a doctor or the emergency room, knowing in my gut that something was terribly wrong? No. Instead, I put on an orthopedic boot—the black thing people wear temporarily after they get off crutches—because it seemed to reduce the bowing a bit. When I got back home to California, I demonstrated for Johnny, grabbing my knee with one hand, the ankle with the other, and pulled the ankle back to bend my leg. And by bending, I mean the bone itself. The tibia.

Together, we went to see Dr. Wiss. I said I thought something might be broken in there and demonstrated the bowing. His eyes widened. He leaned back. He put a hand over his face. And he said in a voice you never want to hear from a doctor, "We need an X-ray."

Five minutes later he arranged the pictures on the light board. It didn't require a doctor's expertise to see that the titanium had broken and leg was in two distinct parts separated by a two-inch gap.

My first thought was, *Okay, so he'll put a cast on it.* Johnny, also not thinking this was any big deal, joked, "Leave it to Amberly to break titanium."

Which raised a good question: "How *do* you break titanium?" I asked.

"The hardware wore out faster than your leg could heal,"

he said, explaining that the plates connecting those pieces were only as good as the speed at which my leg could heal (without a bone graft). The metaphor he used was of a huge tree with a thick bough. If you yank on that bow nothing's going to happen right away. But if you keep pulling down on that bough, day after day, eventually it's going to weaken and then, seemingly suddenly, snap. That's what happened with my titanium plates.

"We're going to have to schedule a surgery."

But this wasn't going to be any surgery. He was going to have to work in conjunction with another surgeon, the one who'd done my plastic surgery, to cut through the muscle flap and open everything up.

It turned out to be the longest surgery of them all—ten hours. It was so long and so complicated that they had to do a second surgery to close my leg up. They then kept me in the hospital for two weeks, in part because Dr. Wiss worried I'd get on my leg and undermine all the hard work. By now he'd gotten to know the kind of person I was, which in fact was the reason he worked so hard during the surgery.

What I later heard from Dr. Wiss—one of the world's foremost trauma surgeons—was that this was *the most difficult surgery he'd ever performed*. They had to take out all the broken titanium pieces and screws, then put the new rod in. Doing that with an intact tibia is hard enough. But this was a shattered tibia. He first tried to put the north end of the rod beneath my kneecap, but it wouldn't go. As an alternative, he had to put it through the knee, underneath the kneecap, then through and down my leg.

Dr. Sherman, the plastic surgeon who had a great sense of humor, laughed when he relayed the story. "Never," he said, "have I seen Dr. Wiss sweat that hard, trying to get that rod in your leg."

It meant a lot to me that it meant so much to him. He'd seen how hard I'd fought to save my leg, and knew the only alternative to his succeeding was amputation. I'm pretty sure any other doctor would have stood at my bedside after I woke from the surgery and, pointing to the stump where my leg used to be, apologized for doing his best but, "Hey, girl, your damn leg just wouldn't cooperate, so we had to take it." Wiss hadn't given up on me. I'll remember that the rest of my life.

It would take two years for the two sides of the bone to grow together. And the thing that, to this day, still astounds every doctor who treated me was I never developed a bone infection of the kind that would've almost certainly required amputation. What I later learned was that there was a 99 percent chance of that happening.

39

I'd Fallen in Love

WHEN I LEFT TEXAS FOR CALIFORNIA after high school graduation, the consensus among my friends was that I'd be back soon for good, and live the kinds of lives they were planning for themselves. They weren't being rude about it, or even envious. But they didn't believe the dreams I had for my life could come true, which was an attitude I never misinterpreted as reflecting on me and my abilities and determination. It was more about their having internalized the moral of the Icarus story: try to fly too high, and you'll crash and burn. In this case, crashing and burning didn't mean dying. It meant returning home to pick up the pieces. So even if they were right, I couldn't see what the harm was in trying. For them, I mean.

For me, I had no intention of crashing and burning; failure wasn't an option. And I quickly proved it, both to me and to them.

Barely six months after leaving, I returned home for a few days at Christmas—and the news of my impending arrival traveled like a shipboard virus. Cars were lined up down the block from Mom's, waiting to say hi. Why? Because the M. C. Hammer video I danced in, the one I'd booked soon after getting to California, was in heavy rotation on MTV. Nobody in town hadn't see it, even adults who'd never have happened on it if not for someone saying, "Wow, that's Amberly."

In the coming years, the townsfolk had many opportunities to see some of my work, including a Melissa Etheridge music video, a Yoshinoya Beef commercial, a Chevy commercial, several infomercials, and an *Elle* glamour spread. Some they didn't see because no one in the States could. One of my favorite gigs was a series of fashion shows I did bi-annually for three years in Japan, where they were (and maybe still are) absolutely infatuated with American pop culture and wanted a row of young American female dancers, particularly blondes with long eyelashes, on the stage to glamorize the proceedings.

I'm sure I'd gotten that gig the first time, and was invited back five subsequent times (spending ten days there each time, being treated wonderfully and shown the sights), because I spoke some of the Japanese words I'd learned while shooting the Yoshinoya commercial to the Japanese producer, who hired me on the spot. In fact, I'm pretty sure that my personality was often more important than my physicality in booking gigs. In my own mind, I was never the best-looking or most talented woman in the lobby where we waited for our auditions. I'd walk in and often wonder what I was doing there. But then, when they met me and I could strike up a conversation with them, they'd do the calculus of what it was going to be like to spend days or weeks working with this particular person who has a pleasant personality versus someone who's better looking but has no sense of humor.

It was on my last trip to Japan, each of which lasted ten days, that I decided it was time for me to be done with this portion of my career and move on to something else. As I mentioned, I always knew that twenty-five was the top age for this job, both mentally and physically, for me. But at the time I hadn't figure on emotionally too. In Japan for those ten days, I missed Savanna so much, and was certain she missed her mommy too. She stayed with her grandmother while I was gone, and all I could think about was how this was no life for either of us.

Yes, I needed the money—very good money, that gig. And I was the only dancer who'd been selected for each of the previous five shows, too, so it was likely I'd be in line for the next one six months down the line. But in six months I wanted to be doing something else because I didn't want to keep leaving Savanna. She was the best thing that had ever happened to me, and was more important than any dance job I could've booked. In fact, she was more important than anything.

Most dancers live in fear of a debilitating injury, same as all professional athletes do. Every dancer knew other dancers who'd ended their careers prematurely because of injuries, especially knee injuries, as what happened to me. I don't even know how it happened; I only remember feeling this pain in my knee that kept me from being my best. Given my pain threshold, I'd probably overlooked it and tried to dance through it much longer than I should have, exacerbating whatever the issue was when it first happened. By the time I felt debilitated enough to see a doctor, he diagnosed a torn meniscus—basically the most common injury. Naturally, I took his advice and scheduled him to do an arthroscopy. And naturally, me being me, I started going to the gym and working out my leg, hoping to get it as strong as possible before the surgery.

What happened after a few weeks at the gym surprised me: My leg began feeling better—so much better, in fact, that

I canceled the surgery, which I wasn't all that crazy about doing in the first place. And then I started thinking, if I can do this kind of thing and get stronger, it would be so incredible to help other people do the same. Two professions did that: physical therapists and personal trainers. Only one of those appealed to me. As a teacher, I'd already had experience working with people, and been working out and running for as long as I could remember.

More to the point, I knew how great exercise made me feel and believed I could share that enthusiasm with others, so that they could get the same feeling and benefits. That's when I started asking around if anyone knew someone who could point me in the right direction to be a physical trainer, and about a week later at a dinner party I mentioned how much I loved everything about fitness and had begun to consider how to be a trainer. One of the women there said her trainer teaches people how to train and volunteered to connect us.

I went to the state-of-the-art gym—the nicest I'd ever seen—and signed up for the eight-week course. When I finished that, I had to pass an intense hands-on exam, then apprentice by shadowing another trainer for months, then the instructor hired me to train him. That's what started me off. From there I hustled for clients by asking the gym if I could volunteer my time to offer free one-hour, one-on-one sessions to all new gym members. I literally picked up the phone and cold called them, and a high percentage said yes to the freebie, and many ended up signing on for more.

I ended up working forty to sixty hours a week, once I started getting word-of-mouth referrals. A lot of my clients were well-to-do people who wanted to be trained in their home gyms, so I did a lot of driving all over the L.A. area. Six mornings a week I taught a group of ladies in Beverly

Hills who'd gather in one woman's home that was something you'd have seen in movies from the 1930s—that kind of splendor and elegance, with a maid answering the door in uniform. To reach the home gym, you had to go out the back door, which was a walk itself, then cross the tennis court to a freestanding building that was more like a clubhouse than a cabana or pool house.

These ladies, most of them in their 60s and 70s, were unforgettable. Full of enthusiasm and spunk, they loved that I was a single mom and hard-working. I would show up to teach aerobics and in return, they would share much of their wisdom. Every year at Christmas they treated Savanna and me to a fancy tea party at the Beverly Hills Hotel. It was at these tea parties Savanna learned how to sit like a lady and have tea with the finest.

I'd train them doing aerobics from seven o'clock till eight-fifteen, then did another couple nearby in Beverly Hills. At nine-thirty, I'd drive back over the hill to North Hollywood, and some days further north and west, to Porter Ranch. But I always ended up back in Woodland Hills at the gym, where I'd taken over the trainer certification course. By then I'd gotten so busy that I had three trainers working for me.

At some point, I tired of all the driving, especially over the hill from the San Fernando Valley to the west side, where Beverly Hills is. It coincided, not coincidentally, with meeting Johnny. I told the ladies about this man I thought I'd fallen in love with, and by their reaction I realized why they loved that I was a single mom and hard-working, trying to raise my daughter—because it meant they could count on me to show up every morning. Some months later, one of them shouted, "There's a ring on your finger!" I said yes, he'd proposed and I'd accepted. They were happy for me, but probably also conflicted, suspecting that they were soon to lose me.

At first I was a little confused at their reactions, then I understood what a compliment it was, and I've thought of it that way ever since. For my next book, I could write about them and what amazing women they are. It would likely be a three-volume set.

40
Counting Every Win

ONE OF THE MOST REMARKABLE PARTS of the surgery that Dr. Wiss performed was getting my leg not only straight, but making it the same length as my other leg. That's a huge deal, as anyone who's ever limped for an extended period can tell you. Limping changes not only your gait; it impacts your whole skeletal system. Over time, a limp leads to severe problems up and down the spine and into every joint. He spent so much time and effort making sure that when I got full use of my right leg again—or as close to full as possible—I wouldn't be saddled with secondary or tertiary problems down the line.

(I know this sounds like a small thing, praising a surgeon for doing his job properly and paying attention to detail, but it isn't. I know another man who'd had a motorcycle accident that required his leg to be in a cast for fourteen months. By the time he got the cast off and rehabbed my leg, it was too late to do anything about the fact that his surgeon—allegedly one of the finest and most expensive orthopods around—had connected his foot to his ankle at an angle, giving him years of spinal and hip issues.)

Before Dr. Wiss inserted the new titanium rod, the pain level was excruciating because every step I took was on a

172 TRUE GRIT and Grace

broken leg. After the new titanium rod was inserted, the pain level was excruciating—but not quite as excruciating. So, I counted that as a win. All I needed to know at any given moment was that the trend was up; things were getting better, not worse. I endured the pain with as much cheerfulness as I could muster, feeling certain the level was well beyond what normal people consider tolerable.

Yes, I had the help of some strong drugs, but they made me feel zoned out. I'd already missed enough time with my little Ruby, and Savanna was about to start high school. That last thing I wanted was to be absent from them mentally now after having been absent physically. That's why, from the beginning, I was intent on weaning myself off the drugs as quickly as possible. If that meant learning to compartmentalize the to get on with my life, then so be it.

For a long time, though, my life was preparing for the next surgery, then the next one, then the next. One of the surgeries was to literally break my ankle and cut a notch in my Achilles tendon because the ankle was frozen and couldn't bend. So getting on with my life was a long series of three steps up (to the degree that I could take steps) and six steps back, both physically and emotionally. Every single one of these surgeries—that eventually totaled about forty—would have been, for most people, a significant, even life-changing, event. For me, they were bumps in the road. I couldn't think of them as anything but that. If I had, I would have given up.

And nothing, not even a doctor's advice, could get me to do that.

41

Something Very Serious

MONTHS AFTER I GOT OUT OF the hospital the first time, I drove to Beverly Hills to see a world-renowned specialist, referred by Dr. Wiss, for a physical assessment of me, my leg, and whatever else. At the time, I was jazzed about being out of the wheelchair and able to get around on crutches. Being able to put my leg down long enough to get from here to there was a very big deal. So, there I sat in his office, feeling incredibly proud as he looked at me, looked at my leg, and reviewed my chart.

And then he abruptly left the room. I turned to Johnny, wondering what was going on. Obviously, he didn't know any more than I did, except we both knew instinctively that this wasn't good.

Sure enough, the doctor came back in and said, "You've got something very serious."

I said, "Okay. And?"

He asked, "Are you the kind of person who tends to push through pain?"

Enthusiastically, I said, "Well, yes, I am."

"Well," he said, "you need to stop doing that right now. You have something called Complex Regional Pain Syndrome."

"What's that?"

"It's a nerve disease. It's serious. It's *very* serious. And it's incurable. You need to go home, get in your wheelchair, put your leg up, keep it up, and stay there."

"For how long?"

"Forever."

"Why"

"Because you're going to be in terrible pain the rest of your life. Your leg will never work properly, and you'll probably never be able to function properly in society as a normal person. You'll always be handicapped."

On and on he went, as if there was anything left to say—not that I was still listening. Pretty much at "never" I checked out. No way was I going to listen anymore to this guy who'd never met me and had no idea who I was or what I was capable or incapable of doing.

All I had been doing since the accident was pushing through the pain. Now here he was telling me to stop. To give up. To give in. To stop moving forward. Or even trying to. Whether I paid attention to the words spewing from his mouth in a torrent, I was already heartbroken. Having survived what I'd survived; having endured what I'd endured; having overcome what I'd overcome to be able to walk myself on crutches into his office only to be told that I had a life-altering, debilitating disease was like a piano dropping out of the Empire State Building onto my head.

Frankly, I didn't know what to do or think. For me, dealing with skeletal and muscular issues, like torn ligaments and broken bones, is a hangnail. But nerve pain is something different. It's the worst kind of pain (as anyone who's ever suffered a bout of sciatica knows) and was not going away, this man said. It would be with me every minute of every day the rest of my life—the life I might, apparently, want to end sooner rather than later, according to the CRPS's sardonic nickname, "The Suicide Disease."

The statistics say that, way disproportionately to the general population, people who must live with CRPS take their own lives after realizing they don't have what it takes to live with it every minute of every day for the rest of their lives. Which means *the rest of their lives* must be shorter than they would have been otherwise.

Taking your life is a choice. But I knew, even as the depression overwhelmed me that morning, suicide would never be my choice.

I didn't say a word to Johnny on the drive home. And when we got home, I let him off and said I had an errand to run. The errand was physical therapy.

I showed up at the therapist's clinic. He said, "You don't have an appointment today."

"I know," I said. "But the doctor told me something today that made me realize I better start working out even harder than I have been."

"Okay," he said, and fit me in.

I cried through the whole workout from pain, but I did it, and I haven't stopped since. In fact, for a long time I was an easy mark for every charlatan, snake-oil salesman, and faith healer—pretty much anyone who promised he or she could, for a fee, get me out of pain. A short list of what I spent a ton of money and time on includes acupuncture and acupressure, spinal blocks, spinal radio frequency, micro-current treatment, ketamine infusions, chiropractic, spinal stimulator, homeopathic medicine, meditation, chakra balancing, and aura clearing.

But somewhere in between surgeries number thirty and

thirty-four I decided I didn't need nerve medication anymore and wondered why the doctors didn't have me drink a glass of red wine every night to ease that stubborn ole nerve pain. I thought it was genius. Who needs meds? The wine not only numbed out my pain but also seemed to help me stuff all those inadequate feelings and suck it up even more. The plan worked until it didn't and my whole life was tumbling down before me. The light that used to shine bright inside me was growing dimmer by the minute.

The drinking became more frequent because one glass stopped working, then two, three, and so on. I was living a double life by trying to pull it together by day and drinking when it was five o'clock somewhere. My world became smaller and I was dying inside. I didn't know if I had tremors because I was having withdrawal from the meds or I was dependent on the alcohol, but it scared me enough to know I needed help and I couldn't suck it up not one more day. I googled alcoholic support groups. Since I was not only hiding my drinking from the world but also hiding how much I was drinking from my very own husband, I would also sneak out to my very first meeting.

Scarier than any of my surgeries was walking in that room for the first time. But for the first time in a long time I was given the gift of hope and a stronger connection to my higher power. The obsession to drink was slowly lifted. I knew for the first time I didn't have to suck it up; what I didn't know was how much better my life was going to get.

March 13, 2016

I confessed to Dr. Rasool today that I had stopped taking my medication cold turkey. I didn't confess to him that I started drinking instead. He was obviously concerned and baffled by my decision. He told me I was lucky I didn't go into full blown seizures because it was an anti-seizure medication for my nerve pain. You have to be slowly weaned off. You can't just stop taking it because your body stops producing the chemicals to combat seizures with this type of medication. My first thought was I could have had a serious accident while driving with Ruby in the car. From that day forward, I stopped playing doctor and listened to my real physician instead.

42

Then Came the Miracle

A FEW WEEKS AFTER I GOT home from the hospital, a friend stopped by. I was lying in the portable bed in my living room. She sat on one corner of it, looked at me, sighed, and asked, "What're you going to do now?"

"What do you mean?"

"I mean, for work. You can't train clients anymore."

That thought hadn't entered my mind for even a second, so to hear a close friend utter the words was excruciating in a whole new way. I burst into tears.

Even in the early days at the hospital, after I'd awakened from the coma, I'd been on my Blackberry, trying to contact every one of my clients and let them know I'd be back soon. At the time I figured a month, then kept extending it as circumstances dictated, which I recognize now was a form of either denial or delusion. I'd spent so much time thinking about them, wanting to do right by them, that one day Johnny snatched the phone out of my hand and yelled, "Enough!"

As it happened, at the moment my friend showed up that day, I had been writing out exercise sheets for every one of my clients. Why? I needed them. I needed them more than they needed me. I needed to get back to work. I needed to give my life purpose above and beyond trying to walk again. Purpose was what was going to save me mentally, psychologically, spiritually—and, for that matter, physically. Purpose was what was going to get me on my feet and, someday—or so I prayed—running again. The rest would follow from there.

When I could reasonably hobble around on crutches or, when that got too painful, push myself around in a wheelchair, one of my clients, Debbie, came over and graciously let me "train" her. I put scare quotes around "train" because it wasn't the way I had trained her in the past. Although I carefully planned her workout, I was training her in my living room with some small dumbbells instead of at the gym with all the different apparatus. It was strange, and I was sure Debbie had agreed to do this out of the kindness of her heart. (She claims to this day that I was incredibly helpful, but I still think she was, and is, only being nice.) After a few sessions, though, I felt jumpstarted and decided to go back to the gym. That required overcoming my touchiness bordering on embarrassment about people seeing me so hobbled (and catching sight of the damaged leg). For a few weeks I did whatever I could to get myself in shape, or at least better shape, ignoring what I feared people were saying or thinking about me in order to concentrate on the task at hand.

One day after I had forgotten to be self-conscious, someone I didn't know (and who didn't know what had happened to me) said, "You know, you really shouldn't walk with a limp. It's bad for your skeletal system."

I had to stifle a laugh. Here I was, finally going from station to station on my own legs, doing my best to ignore the pain and get on with the program—which in itself was its own kind a miracle she couldn't have known about—and she couldn't help sticking her officious nose in my business. I said, "You're right. As soon as my leg's not broken anymore, I plan to ditch the limp."

Despite my sarcastic response, I was pleased that I'd progressed to the point where a stranger wasn't pitying me for the obvious catastrophe I'd survived; she was treating me like someone able-bodied. Still, the hidden message of what she said struck a sore spot with me. Namely, *Who's going to want to train with me? I'm broken.*

But then came the miracle. Business began booming, and did so quickly. Why? Because people saw me in the gym, in my wheelchair or on crutches, and it sparked something in them. The sight of me with my leg bandaged, walking with a limp, or being on crutches, even pushing myself to some stations in a wheelchair, was somehow inspirational. People would come up to me and say that they'd awakened that morning not wanting to work out, or go to spinning class, or whatever, but then they'd remember me and decide, *Hey, if that lady can do it, I don't have any excuses.*

Even as the boom was happening, I could hardly believe how fast things were moving. Anyone trying to overcome some physical issue or hurdle—for instance, a back injury or arthritis—now sought me out. Those who'd been told, *you can't*, now heard from me, *Oh, yes you can*, and that was how I trained them.

A client whom I'd trained longer than anyone, about twenty years, said that I was a better trainer for her now than I'd been before the injury. Now, she said, I have a better understanding of her pain and her limitations because of what I experienced. Without doing so consciously, I'd developed a new kind of empathy that allowed me to approach the work through my clients' eyes and bodies.

As a consequence of all that, my clientele changed. It was

kind of magic. The tractor beam created by my new purpose in life attracted people who also saw in training a way to support their own purposes, whatever they might be. And though I'd intended to take on only a few clients, the cascade eventually had me working more hours than I ever had. Yes, the toll on my leg was sometimes rough. More often, what would have been otherwise unendurable was doable because I felt as if I were serving people.

So now there was only one more hurdle for me to jump over. Literally.

43

Notice the Gifts

I WRITE DOWN IN MY JOURNAL what I'm grateful for. True, it's mostly the same list every day—my family, my friends, my leg, that I'm learning to belly dance, the new rose blooms in my backyard, my sobriety, etc.—though sometimes the list on a day when the pain is a real ten might be noting how grateful I am that yesterday's pain was only an eight.

If that sounds insane or impossible, consider what the alternative is. Besides, back when I was crawling up the steps, I felt grateful for the chance to be in my own closet and pick out my own clothes. So I'd better be grateful for being able to stand, even in pain, walk up and down the stairs, and get from here to anywhere all on my own.

What I've learned is life is a series of choices we make regardless of our circumstances. I could either make the choice to give up and let my life be determined *by* my circumstances or fight to create something positive *out of* my circumstances. My choice is to get up and do the best I can each day. My choice is to notice the gifts life offers, which are particularly plentiful when you look for them. My choice is to be happy. I believe in angels. I believe we have the power to see good in every situation and learn from it.

It's ironically fitting that the story of my leg begins with running. Had I not taken that long run that fateful morning, and the stars lined up just right, I wouldn't have even been in the wrong place at the wrong time when that man pulled out of the driveway.   But as you probably noticed, I was something of a maniac about running.

As long as I can remember, since even before I joined the track and cross country teams for my school, I'd loved to run. In fact, that was why I'd taken up running in school. At the time, my love of running was a combination of feeling free and working things out emotionally. Running was my therapy. And the endorphins it created were my Prozac. Of course, at the time, I had no idea what real therapy was or that there was even such a thing as a drug that affected your mood. I knew that running would never not make me feel better. Yes, I loved dancing, and dancing made me feel good, but sometimes I even ran after dancing.

So when there was a question of whether I'd ever be able to walk again after the accident, one of the things I worried about was what would happen to me if I couldn't run. Seriously. In my mind, whatever issues I would have dealt with by not being able to walk would have been mitigated had I been able to run. Don't try to untangle the contradiction; it can't be done. I knew what running had done, and could do, for me in all the worst times.

At last, after I ditched my crutches for good, and was training clients on my own two legs, and exercising myself the way I wanted to, I vowed that I would run again too. Instead of asking *Why me*, I asked, *What's next....*

February 20, 2013.

I did it. I finally did it. I ran today with Ruby at the beach. I ran until I fell flat in the sand, then got up and did it again. We ran all afternoon. It was one of the best days of my life.

44

Just the Way You Are

AFTER THE TEN-HOUR SURGERY DR. WISS performed to take out the broken pieces of titanium and replace them with a rod, I, of course, called the pathology department to ask if I could have all that metal. After all, according to what was billed to our insurance company, it was approximately $62,000 worth of titanium, and I was planning on keeping it to make a couple of bracelets, one for Savanna and one for Ruby. After my millionth call to the pathology department, I think they finally got sick of me and agreed to send it to my hospital room.

To my surprise, the collection didn't come in a cute little gift bag, but a gallon-sized plastic bag filled with two long pieces of metal and about twenty-five screws that still had reminisce of blood. Some of the screws were about three inches in length, some only one inch, and most were broken. It looked more like something you would find at a hardware store rather than a hospital.

When I was finally able to do things on my own again, I cleaned the metal and made a trip down to the local jewelry store to see about having those bracelets made. Unfortunately, the jeweler informed me the bracelets couldn't be made because the metal was too hard to bend. I was left feeling a little disappointed, but at the same time a little like a superhero for breaking the metal in the first place.

A long time passed and I had almost forgotten about the bag of broken metal completely. But one day, I decided to do some spring cleaning and found the crumpled bag tucked all the way in the back of my desk, and an idea came to mind. I gathered some fishing line, a few beautiful feathers I had collected to remind me of my guardian angel Big Granny, a sparkly crystal, the piece of driftwood Johnny had given me engraved with, "I love you just the way you are," and all the broken titanium. I sat outside and enjoyed the warm sunlight on my face and the smell of our sweetheart rose bush that was in full bloom. I tied the feathers, crystal, and broken pieces of titanium to the driftwood to create the most unique and expensive wind chime I had ever seen. I was so proud.

I hung it under the lemon tree where I knew I would be able to see and hear it most. I then sat back and took notice of how the feathers danced with the slight breeze and I listened to the beautiful, sweet sound the titanium that once held my leg together now made. It reminds me that difficult roads often lead to beautiful destinations and in life sometimes it takes a little grit along with God's grace to get through the most challenging times. And ever since that fateful day on my motorcycle, life has often been so difficult and so painful at times, but I have transformed into the best version of myself despite it all.

So yes, I am grateful I can run, even if it's not the way I used to, and not as often. But more than anything, I am grateful for the positive shift in my perspective, the faith and hope I've found, and the courage to get back up time and time again. This wind chime reminds me to touch my wounds with forgiveness and view my scars as a symbol of battles I have

won. Once you own your story and embrace your imperfections, you can learn to have acceptance and then begin to
truly heal and be comfortable in your own skin.

I have learned to pray and my relationship with God is
stronger. I have learned I never have to do anything alone.
I have learned the true meaning of resilience. It comes from
deep within us and from the support around us. True resilience is finding the courage to move forward and choosing to
live a life filled with laughter and love even when things don't
go as planned. It is possible to regain confidence and joy.
What I know now is anything is possible.

What lies behind us and what lies before us are tiny matters
Compared to what lies within us.
—HENRY STANLEY HASKINS

Acknowledgements

THANK YOU DR. WISS AND DR. JABOUR for your skilled expertise, genuine kindness, and for never giving up on me or my leg. To all my other doctors and nurses along the way, for without you these words would never have appeared on paper.

Joel Engel, thank you for saving the day with your expertise and advice on writing, insight and guidance, and for continually telling me that my story should be heard.

Jack Grapes, my writing instructor who told me that one day I *would* write a book.

My amazing editor, Anna Floit, for your loving red pen, kind words, and patience.

To the phenomenal team of people at Morgan James Publishing, I am in awe of the professionalism, talent, and confidence you have shown my story. I thank you for bringing my dream to life.

My family and friends who have been by my side every step of the way. I know it wasn't easy and it did take a village. I love you and I am full of gratitude for each of you. My powerful goddess women warriors and spiritual teachers, every single one of my clients, my entire belly dance tribe, my sponsor and sobriety sisters, and Bob and Marilyn who are my adopted California family.

Thank you to my mom and dad for being who you are because you made me who I am, and Granny for being my role model.

And for being my inspiration, my life, my loves…for being my everything, I thank you, Johnny, Savanna, and Ruby.

With all the love in my heart,
Amberly

True Grit and Grace Together

BY COMING TOGETHER AND SUPPORTING ONE another, we can forge onward and find the strength to persevere.

I invite you to visit my website, *AmberlyLago.com*, and connect with me there.

For daily inspiration, join me on:

Facebook: @amberlylagomotiationalspeaker
Instagram: @amberlylagomotivation
Twitter: @amberlylago

Morgan James
Speakers Group

↗ www.TheMorganJamesSpeakersGroup.com

We connect Morgan James published
authors with live and online events
and audiences who will benefit
from their expertise.

CPSIA information can be obtained
at www.ICGtesting.com
Printed in the USA
BVHW03s0845200318
511070BV00001B/39/P

9 781683 506232